COMMERCIAL SPACES

Shops, Malls and Boutiques

COMMERCIAL SPACES

Shops, Malls and Boutiques

B. T. Batsford Ltd • London

AUTHOR
Francisco Asensio Cerver

PUBLISHING DIRECTOR
Paco Asensio

PROJECT COORDINATOR
Rosa Maria Prats

PROOFREADING
Carola Moreno
A.B.C. Traduccions

TRANSLATION
A.B.C. Traduccions

© Copyright for International edition
AXIS BOOKS, S.A.

© Copyright for English edition
ROTOVISION

ISBN 0 7134 7867 5

First published in
Great Britain 1995
Published by B.T. Batsford Ltd
4 Fitzhardinge Street
London W1H 0AH

No part of this publication may be reproduced, stored in retrieval system or transmitted in any form or by any means, electronic, mechanical, photocopying, recording or otherwise, without the prior written permission of the owner of the copyright.

Without any doubt at all the hardest part of an introduction, such as the present one, is the justification of the parameters of selection and classification which have been employed. In the multi-faceted and fertile panorama of sales spaces, the choice of a few determined projects exemplifying the current state of commercial design is crucial to any work which wishes to combine both visual quality and informative rigour. However, the variety offered by, and the creative lucidity of, a few of the most prestigious architects/designers working in present-day interior design have rendered the task of selecting the projects, which are illustrated in this book, a relatively easy one.

The exercise of taxonomy is, in another sense, much riskier given that, in this complex pre-millennial age, categories and divisions are losing their traditional significance, giving way to combinations, blends and syntheses of tendencies, concepts and functions. This consideration is specifically relevant to the subject of commercial spaces, where the importance of the leisure-consumerism duality is reflected as one of the motors which drives our economic and social relations in the present day.

The intention of these introductory reflections is to justify the structure of the present work, which is divided into three independent, and at the same time, complementary sections. As a result it is possible to detect certain conceptual cross currents, as well as certain formal connections which only serve to corroborate the sense of disorder and confusion which preside over contemporary times.

The central block, corresponding to commercial centres, is the one which has afforded the fewest difficulties for classification. The parameters which characterise these spaces are fairly obvious: large-scale display and sales areas, which offer a plurality and variety of product, and the concentration of the greatest possible number of customer services.

However, the option has been taken in this edition to avoid, what has been the most ubiquitous of commercial phenomena over the last few decades, the macro-spaces which have inevitably had an impoverishing effect. The macro-spaces have mercilessly imposed a monumental and monolithic hierarchy without reference to the urban context, putting lucrative ends over and above the least regard for environmental considerations. In their stead projects have been included which demonstrate that large scale interventions can be naturally integrated into the urban fabric, and can serve as a focus for the architecture and the socio-cultural dynamism of the town or city. This is the case, for example, with Stockholm Södra, by DOM-Borowski Arkitekter AB, or of the commercial and hotel centre in Hamm, by Brigitte and Christoph Parade.

In the other two sections of this book, those dealing with shops and boutiques, the difficulties of classification are considerably increased. One determining factor has served, from a conceptual point of view, to place them in a group; that is the intention expressed through them to react against the impersonal massification associated with large and anodyne commercial spaces. The desire to create singular and individualised spaces with their own identity is however not only a reaction, it has also become a strategy of inducement (clearly endorsed through its success) for a clientele attracted by all that which is personal and innovative.

There are two systems to bring about this creation of identity; one is the obsessive repetition of iconographic elements, and the other, the configuration of an image defined as corporative, yet which reflects the idiosyncrasies and the spirit of the company. Through the creation of an identifying image any chain of shops, without their being a multinational, or any individual shop can accede to the highest levels of aesthetic and functional quality. The possibilities offered by interior design have erupted with startling force in the field of commercial spaces. The seeds of this movement were originally sewn in the style and fashion sector. The most important creative textile firms understood the need for the items they produced to be displayed in a space which would match their inherent quality, this gave rise to what has become known as the boutique.

This tendency has become progressively incorporated into the majority of sales and commercial sectors. Nowadays there are very few products which do not avail themselves of a corporate image to guarantee their diffusion and maximise their market potential. For this reason Commercial Spaces endeavours to be of service as a help to both professionals working in this field, and also, for all of those who are interested in outstanding architectural and interior design work. The projects included in this book are no more than a sample of the spectacular creativity of the moment which is being experienced in this fascinating area of commercial activity.

SHOPS

10	LA BOTTEGA DI SAN VALENTINO	*Luigi Lanaro & Massimo Cocco*
20	TRUCCO, BILBAO	*Joseba Beranoaguirre*
30	HIGH-TECH	*Mauro Bacchini.*
36	ADDICIONAL	*Lluís Pau, Josep Martorell, Oriol Bohigas & David Mackay*
46	SHOEBALLOO SHOESHOP	*Borek Sipek*
54	FOCHE MAINA	*Manuel Ybargüengoitia & Maria del Mar Nogués*
64	SHU UEMURA	*Jean Louis Veret & Gerard Ronzatti, of Atelier des Ouvriers Reunis*
70	LORCA CRAFT CENTRE	*Juan Antonio Molina*

MALLS

76	COMMERCIAL AND HOTEL CENTRE IN HAMM	*Brigitte & Christoph Parade*
84	STOCKHOLM SÖDRA	*DOM-Borowski Arkitekter AB*
94	COLLIER CAMPBELL	*Michael Brown, Stephen Ibbotson & Anthony Charnley*
104	SHOWROOM CASSINA JAPAN	*Mario Bellini*

BOUTIQUES

114	THE THIERRY MUGLER BOUTIQUE	*Patrick Philippi*
124	ISSEY MIYAKE	*David Chipperfield Architects*
130	EKSEPTION	*Eduard Samsó*
136	SBAIZ SPAZIO MODA	*Claudio Nardi*
144	KENZO	*Maurizio Peregalli*
152	SHOWROOM MARCATRÉ	*King & Miranda Associati*

Shops

La Bottega di San Valentino

Luigi Lanaro & Massimo Cocco

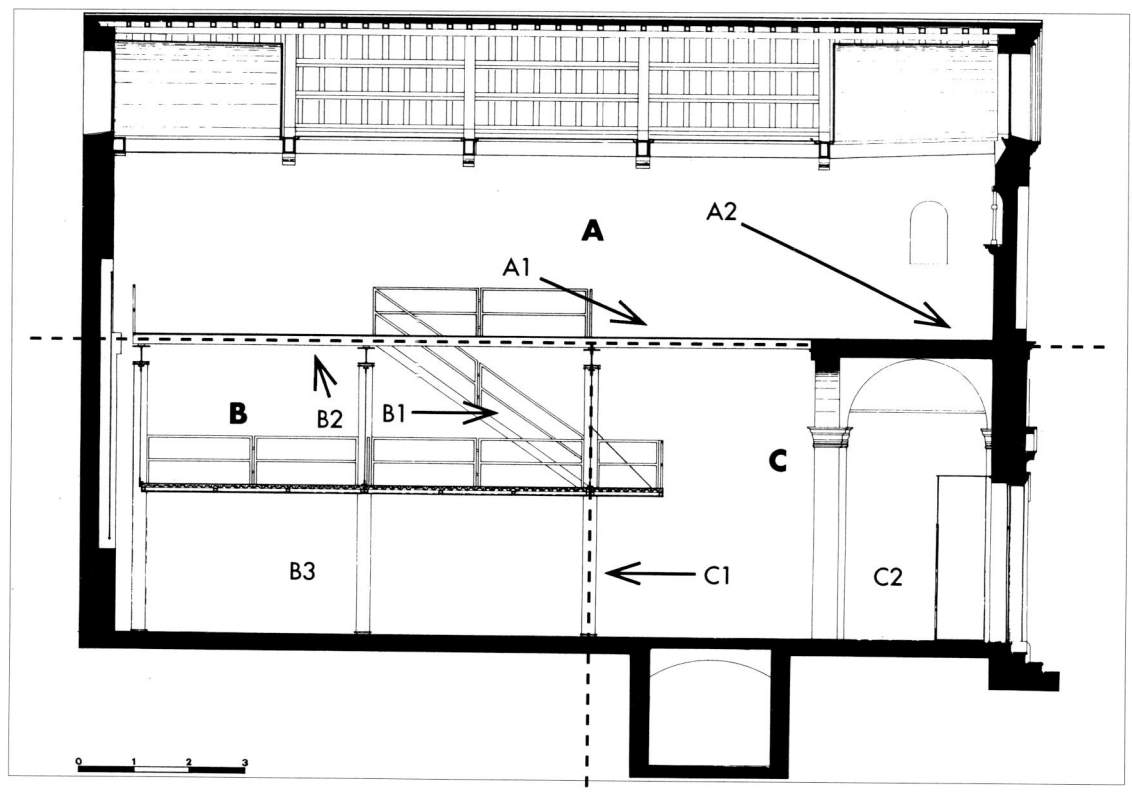

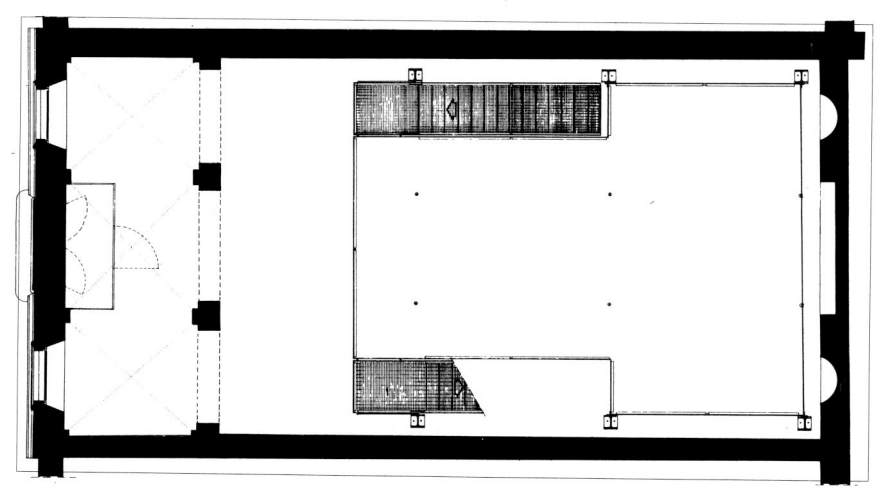

Plan view of the building and elevation plan, divided into sectors A, B and C.

Frontal view of the façade, after its restoration.

The proliferation, over the last ten years, of commercial macro-spaces – a logical by-product of business structures, where the lucrative end is prized above all –, supposes a risk of "massification" and the depersonalisation of the act of buying. When faced with these great spaces, the traditional concept of the shop has had to evolve, in search of alternative procedures to those of size and practicality, to be able to conserve its position as a classical place of commercial transaction, and also of personal interrelations.

In this way, and in opposition to the immense multi-centres, arises the desire to distinguish and personalise the shop premises. With this in view, certain identification procedures have arisen; one of which, probably the most subtle, fertile and creative, is the staging of ambiences which convert an available commercial space into the reflection of the personality of the company, of the product on sale, or even the creativity of the company's designer.

An evident and also a happy example of this line of action, is the work realised by the Italians Luigi Lanaro (Vicenza 1928) and Massimo Cocco (Livorno 1949) on the old church of San Valentino de Vicenza, an authentic breath of fresh and innovative air within the panorama of the creation of commercial spaces. This religious building, after being subject to a sensitive and respectful restoration, now houses between its ancestral walls, not only a commercial premise, but also a modern and pragmatic cultural centre. In this way the authors have recovered the original sense of the term bottega, as a place for experimenting, of confrontation, of ideas and sensations.

The humanist training of one of the authors of this project, Luigi Lanaro, is not something that is separate from this proposal. When he was 29, he interrupted his studies in philosophy to form the Lanaro Arredamenti srl., one of the first companies in Italy to propose a selection of contemporary design for the activity of interior decoration; this vocation also led him to investigate in depth in the field of the architecture of interiors. He is the author of numerous works in his native town, Vicenza, the restoration and decoration of the Palazzo Leoni Montanari, head office of the Banco Ambrosiano Veneto, or the Sala Consiliaria, of the Provincial Administration, being the most significant. Massimo Cocco, for his own part, studied engineering and architecture, and although in the beginning his work was in the area of architectural restoration, at present he works as a project engineer, for the company Lanaro Arredamenti srl., sharing responsibilities with Lanaro himself for the company's main projects.

Returning to the project which concerns us, the work must be considered as an attempt to harmonise the architectural and aesthetic structure of the old building with the commercial needs of space and design, and to recuperate the original values of the religious construction, within a modern scheme that is respectful towards them. It is interesting to highlight the unification of functional propositions and a cultural spirit which benefits the contemplative and reflective process, without

Stairway, communicating the top level of the building. (B1)

Rear area of the interior of the church, where we can observe the division into three height levels, proposed by the stairway. (C1)

General aspect of the entrance (C2).

being limited to the external design of the project. The origin of the work was the remodelling of the church of San Valentino, built in 1586, and threatened with ruin in 1989, the year in which the rehabilitation was begun. The aim was to convert it into a retail sales centre for decorative objects and furniture, for the projection and execution of interior design. The church was successively a religious centre, a hospital, a home for beggars and a store for pharmaceutical products, in this way losing its ecclesiastical character. Luigi Lanaro acquired it for use as a studio, but the need to concentrate the activities of the company Lanaro Arredamenti srl. and to create an exhibition space in tune with the spirit of the company was the impulse which led to the initiation of the remodelling process.

The passage of time and the multiple interventions to which the church had been subjected during its more than 400 years of history, had caused an almost total degradation of the small church. For that reason the first objective was the restoration and recuperation of the original structure of the building, eliminating the subsequent additions which had nothing to do with it. The work of recuperation and refurbishing of the frescos of the main façade and the interiors, which were also very deteriorated, was also carried out.

Subsequently, the objective was to create a mixed and multi-functional space valid for both the holding of cultural activities attracting limited attendances (book presentations, concerts), and also exhibitions (of furniture, architectural document samples, etc.).

The first phase of the intervention was centred on the work of rehabilitation, specifically the resolution of a series of principal problems: the demolition of four pilasters added at the beginning of the century, the recuperation of the painted murals (damaged by damp in the walls), and the original flooring, and finally the definition of the installation of central heating, for the walls with frescos.

After previously testing the structural frame of the building, the pilasters were demolished, without the stability of the building being affected; in order to allow the perimeter walls to breathe, some areas were left opened up, the remaining spaces being clad with a lightly coloured finish, avoiding tints that in time could cause scaling.

The restoration of the paintings on the façade was realised according to the current standards, with limited interventions to complete the most damaged images, the reading of which was still possible. The original flooring was replaced with material that was identical to the original, burned bricks being chosen and also alternate colour schemes.

The initial architecture of the building was simple: a rectangular plane, with an atrium entrance over a triple arcade of bevelled vaults. On this basis a wooden separating structure was made use of, creating a double level, and allowing an intermediate steel plat-

View of the main entrance from the top floor. (A1)

Wooden separating structure between the two first height levels, seen from below. (B2)

Panoramic view of the right hand side of the entrance, seen from above, where we can appreciate the vaulted structure of the building, and also part of the arcade. (A2)

Detail of one of the frescos on the walls, after restoration.

form to be placed between this and the floor, installed without its coming into contact with the perimeter walls, giving the whole a sense of weightlessness and lightness, favouring the overhead diffusion of the light. Likewise, the roofing was given a shape which would allow it to capture as much of the natural light that flooded in through the upper arches as possible. Through these procedures, the authors managed to achieve a considerable display surface, taking advantage of the available space through the harmonisation of the old religious structure and the present design.

All of the materials have been used in their natural state, as is fitting for the recuperation of the old memory of the building. The conservation of the old wooden beams (walnut and beech) offers a contrasting balance to the steel of the platform and the supporting pieces. Together with these elements, the mixture of lime and sand smoothly pigmented for the walls, the bricks of the flooring and the coconut fibre matting, constitute the overall image of the interior, to which a combination of original composition pieces and examples of modern design must also be added.

Area of the top floor, where we can appreciate the wooden ceiling and the recuperation work on the drawings and paintings on the walls. (A)

Detail sketch.

Corner of the first floor, under the metallic platform, where we can appreciate the materials used in the restoration of the walls and the flooring. (B3)

The use of natural light, gentle and diffuse, is one of the key factors in the creation of a suggestive atmosphere, offering a sober, and at the same time fascinating atmosphere, in tune with the overall spirit of the project.

Definitively, the work of Luigi Lanaro and Massimo Cocco finished in January 1990, has become not only an exhibition and sales space, but also a magisterial, humanist and harmonic example of the recuperation and maintenance of old structures, to allow for their later integration into modern urban spaces. The combination of the ancient memory of the religious building, the techniques of modern design and this project's wealth of values, grant to the office of the architect and the interior designer, in works such as this, the category of artist, offering a space which is propitious for the reflection of how commercial activity, although still important, does not constitute the essential function.

Aspect of the second floor, where we can observe the distribution of the metallic platform which sustains it. (B1)

Trucco, Bilbao

Joseba Beranoaguirre

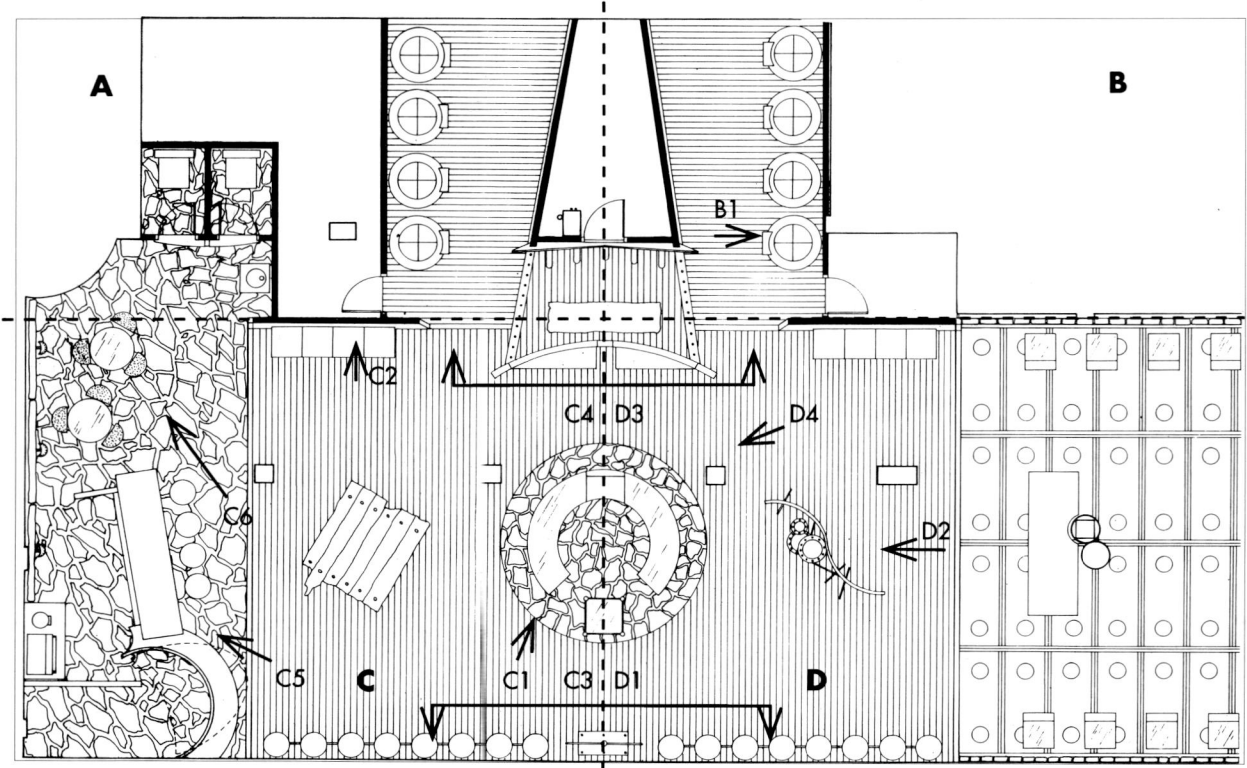

Plan view of the premises, where we can appreciate the distribution of the two distinct sectors of the shop.

The young Basque designer Joseba Beranoaguirre is currently one of the most intuitive authors and innovators in Spanish interior design. Only 30 years old, he has realised designs for a whole variety of interiors and tendencies; fashion shops, shoeshops, driving schools, boutiques and offices have been the vehicles for the moulding of his creative talent, a talent that has become internationally recognised with the publication of his projects in prestigious magazines, such as the German Architektur & Wohnen.

The project which we present here is the shop for the company Trucco, dedicated to the sale and distribution of clothing and footwear, in Bilbao, it was realised in 1990, after he had also worked on the design for another establishment for the same company in Madrid. The development of the project was not easy, due to a series of spatial, economic, standardisation and chronological contingencies which, to a great degree conditioned it, but which Beranoaguirre, through his ingenuity and creativity, was capable of overcoming. Besides, the obligatory influence of the company's commercial identification codes, present in the other shops in Madrid and Pamplona, meant yet another conditioner. A similar interior atmosphere had to be created, based on criteria of distribution and lighting, and in the reiterated use of the company's anagram.

The distribution of space passed through the revision of certain classical concepts concerning the distinct sectors of shops, of which the most significant are those referring to the

Aspect of the central counter, of a circular form, and the cupola above. (C1)

Glass display cases, and behind them the wall of weathered wood, with adornments made from junk-yards and salvaged materials. (C2)

Plan of detail.

String of hangers divided by a capriciously shaped mirror. (C3, D1)

On the following page, an aspect of one part of sector C of the premises, where we can appreciate the great variety of materials and decorative elements employed.

Another perspective of the shop, with an original display of wood in the foreground, and the bar counter behind. (D2)

Fitting cubicles area. (C4, D3)

entrance, the display window and the display. The attempt has been made to introduce a novel aspect, which has not been exactly over-exploited in the Spanish commercial panorama: that of putting a bar inside the shop, as yet another inducement to a purely commercial function.

The author centred his work on the objective of making each of the sectors of the shop perfectly identifiable: the entrance, the central body destined for clothes sales, – and on the basis of which the sections destined as the conveniences, the bar and the store would be distributed –, and finally a space for the sale of footwear. Despite this separation of sectors the author maintains a uniform spirit throughout the interior, underlined by the design and the lighting.

The entrance is spectacular, favoured by a development of great scope and originality;

In the above photo, another perspective of the fitting cubicle area. (A)

The photo below, an aspect of the central counter, where we can see, at the top of the cupola, the blue-toned neon lights which identify the shop's lighting. (D4)

The bar counter, located in one of the lateral areas of the premises. (C5)

for example, the space between the street and the sales area is open, with a notable absence of physical obstacles, allowing for a view, from the exterior, of almost the entire shop. Old pieces of industrial scrap sustain eight glass tubes, inside which articles of clothing are displayed. Two mannequins, and a small XVIII century altar, in oak with mouldings, are the only elements, in this space, which remind us of the classical concept of the display window.

The colour materials and textures, with their economic simplicity, lit in an absolutely suggestive way, manage to introduce us, little by little into the main space of the shop, which consists of an imaginative and insinuating setting.

This space is composed of two rectangular sub-spaces, of different sizes and directions, perpendicular to each other. The first, a prolongation of the entrance area, is the main nucleus of the shop, set aside for the sale of articles of clothing, and the second designed for the sale of footwear.

The surface area for clothing is articulated around an epicentre, formed by the counter

Part of the bar area. (C6)

Aspect of the fitting cubicles. (B1)

situated at the height of the intersection between the shop's two sub-spaces. It is of a circular design, realised with oxidised steel sheeting and aged brass, with a glass covered section for the display of costume jewellery. The cupola which overhangs this element is of scagliola, in natural earth coloured hues; the adjacent lantern comes from a Madrid antique dealer, and was originally meant for the lighting of a vestibule.

The displays are defined by means of the reiterated use of junk-yard material and antiques salvaged from old lofts, plus there is a mirror with a highly stylised shape, this being an original piece designed by Beranoaguirre himself, which overlooks the central counter. The lack of height, and the legal restrictions applicable to commercial premises located on the ground floor of a building prevent the air-conditioning installations from being hidden away, as a result of which the choice was made to maintain the tubing in full view, giving it the greatest possible expressiveness, yet always maintaining the harmony of the overall tone of the establishment.

The footwear area is differentiated by a change in levels of some 17 cm., and the variation in the direction of the wooden flooring strips. This space is divided into two symmetrical areas, in which the fitting cubicles are located: eight independent cylindrical bodies, with oak-wood doors, irregularly marked and streaked, authentic masterpieces salvaged from the junk-yard.

In the bar area, the flooring and part of the walls are made of quartzite, while kiln bricks have been used for the bar, and for the tables, gear wheels from old disused conveyor belts. The bar storage area has been disguised by an inverted gold painted cupola. The most outstanding characteristic of the washrooms, apart from the use of wood and quartzite is the use of a type of tiling, inspired by Gaudí.

The lighting is one of the bases of the personality of the premises; the key criteria being indirect diffusion, almost always towards the ceiling and through the use of neon and halogen spots, which attempt to outline the basically blue colour scheme which dominates the setting.

The innate creative style of this young Basque designer is, then, definitively confirmed

The rear of the premises, which coincide with the fitting cubicle area. (B)

with this new work for the company Trucco, the result of an audacious combination of the modern and the old, with a selection of salvaged and junk-yard components which give it a singular air. The strategy of distribution used to create different spaces with a homogenous atmosphere is also outstanding, in tune with the commercial spirit of the company, and the revision which is made of certain of the classical concepts of the shop, which until now have been almost immovable in the Spanish commercial panorama. Projects such as this one demonstrate how, through creativity and ingenuity, it is possible to resolve a good many of the problems inherent in any work of interior design, and create works of both technical and artistic quality.

Hangers and displays for the different clothing articles, with original decorative motifs. (C, D)

HIGH-TECH

Mauro Bacchini

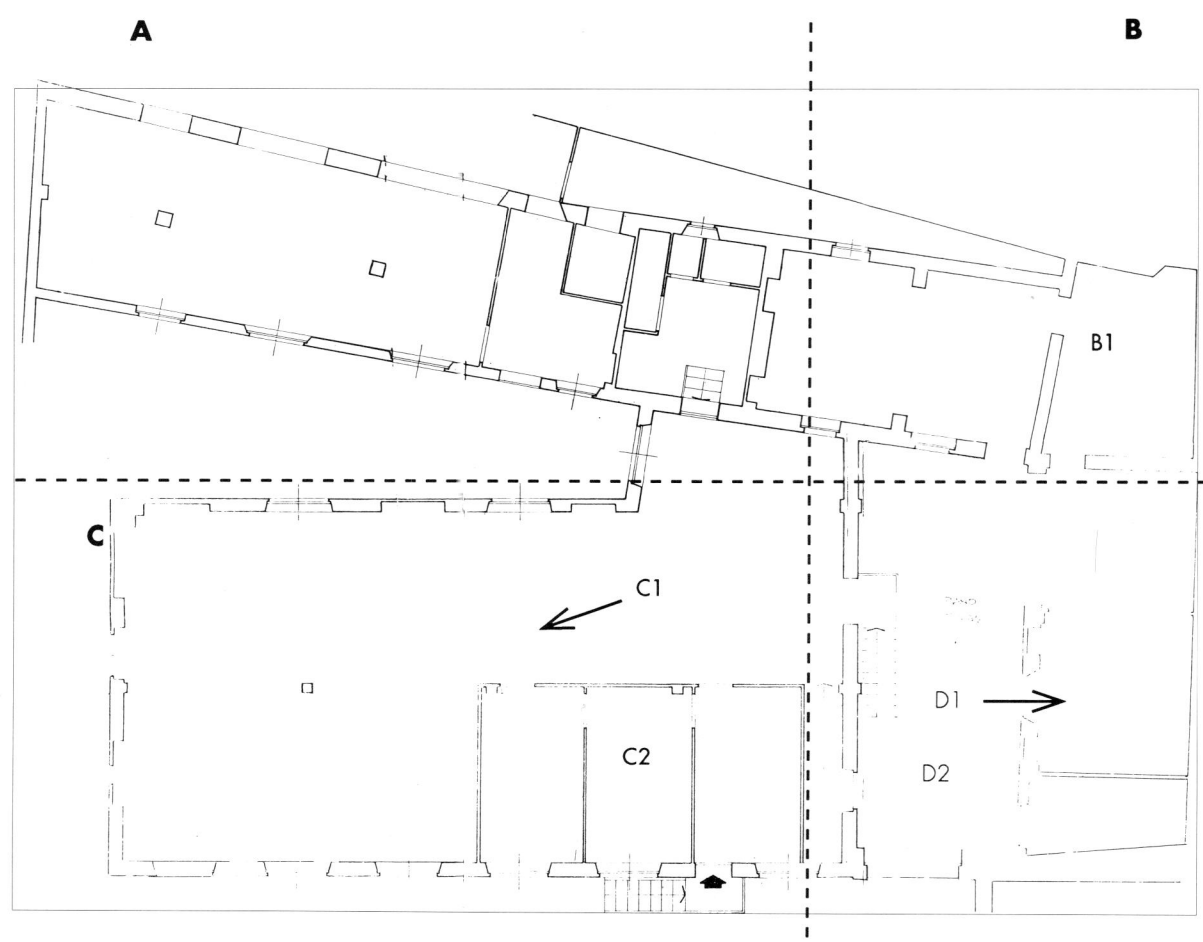

Plan view of the building and the distribution of the different sectors.

Over the last few years an increasing interest has been awoken in the average citizen with regards to the acquisition of objects, not only for their functionality but also for their design and creativity. That is why in many cities shops have opened which renounce the exclusivity of one author or a determined trade mark, in favour of a plural and wider ranging offer, which includes all of the latest creative tendencies.

These commercial propositions reaffirm the classic role of the emporium as a place of transactions, with a cosmopolitan character, and renounce the monopoly of a single company, thus admitting the middle class into the world of the most up-to-date design.

With this in mind, in 1982 High-Tech, a sales and production centre in Milan created by the architect Mauro Bacchini was inaugurated. This multi-faceted author, as well as being a founding member of this company dedicated to design and technological innovation, is also pursuing a career in education in the Domus Academy in the Lombard capital. At the end of 1989 the company's new premises opened its doors, and with the passage of time it has come to be seen as one of the most interesting spaces in the city, not only for the high quality of its products (close to 7,300 articles proceeding from various authors and countries), but also for Bacchini's interior design.

Based on the industrial structure of an old factory, an open commercial space was elaborated, in which the customer, the service and the selection of articles have identical impor-

Corner of the premises, used as a small office. (B1)

Detail of the progression between one room and another, in the basement of the building, where we can appreciate a set of distributing partitions and the clarity of the light which enters from above. (D1)

tance. Thought of as a "small big store", the restructuring of the nave has been based on discretion, an economy of means and the absence of ornamentation, so as, in this way, to concede the maximum protagonism to the perception of the product, and to the circulation of the customers around the premises. The overall ambience of the enclosure has been achieved thanks to the naturalness of the materials and the almost integral diffusion of the outside light, creating a neutral, and at the same time an elegant frame, which enormously favours the possibilities of display.

The building is structured on three floors, at different heights; the non correspondence between street level and the mezzanine floor has allowed for the organisation of the space with a distribution of openings which in turn allowed for the provision of an integral diffusion of natural light to the building, even in the vaulted underground area. The absence of architectural barriers, which would obstruct the natural circulation of the public, is another

Different aspects of the small office area, also used as an exhibition area. (B1)

of the essential characteristics of the premises. Through these means it has come to fulfil its precise function as the ideal container for the articles which are on display, offering all of its constructive qualities (luminosity, extension, organisational clarity) to the service of the concept originated by the author.

The basic characteristics of the main floor, as with the other floors, are made specific by the spaciousness, the chromatic clarity of the constructive elements and the luminosity, entering from the exterior. The stairs have a merely practical function, without any pretense of protagonism.

A series of mezzanine floors and levels which favour the distribution of the sales areas have been created, avoiding, as far as possible, the presence of constructive barriers which would impede circulation.

Functions, such as the production of the company itself and the private areas, are located on the second level. The top floor acts as a furniture exhibition department, and is one of the cosiest sectors in the building. The rustic wood floor, the visible brick facings, the sloping roof with its wooden beams and

Plans of the room set aside for kitchen furniture. (D2)

Top floor of the premises, in the form of a small garret, and detail plan of originally designed chairs. (C2)

the exquisite effect of a shaft of light from directly above the entrance strengthening this sense of ambience, all contribute to the effect.

The basement also offers specific characteristics, such as the vaulted ceiling, which is an original architectural feature; here kitchen utensils, dishes and other domestic articles are on display.

Bacchini's work in High-Tech is a work of compromise with the present age, in two senses. Firstly, in the conceptual sense, with the creation of a space according to the needs of an average public, which is increasingly more intelligent and sensitive, and secondly, in the formal sense, by creating a constructive language, which allows for the development of extensive display and sales surfaces, without the resultant renunciation of a cosy and suggestive atmosphere.

Exhibition of furniture for sitting/dining rooms. (C1)

Addicional

Ll.Pau, J.Martorell, O.Bohigas & D.Mackay

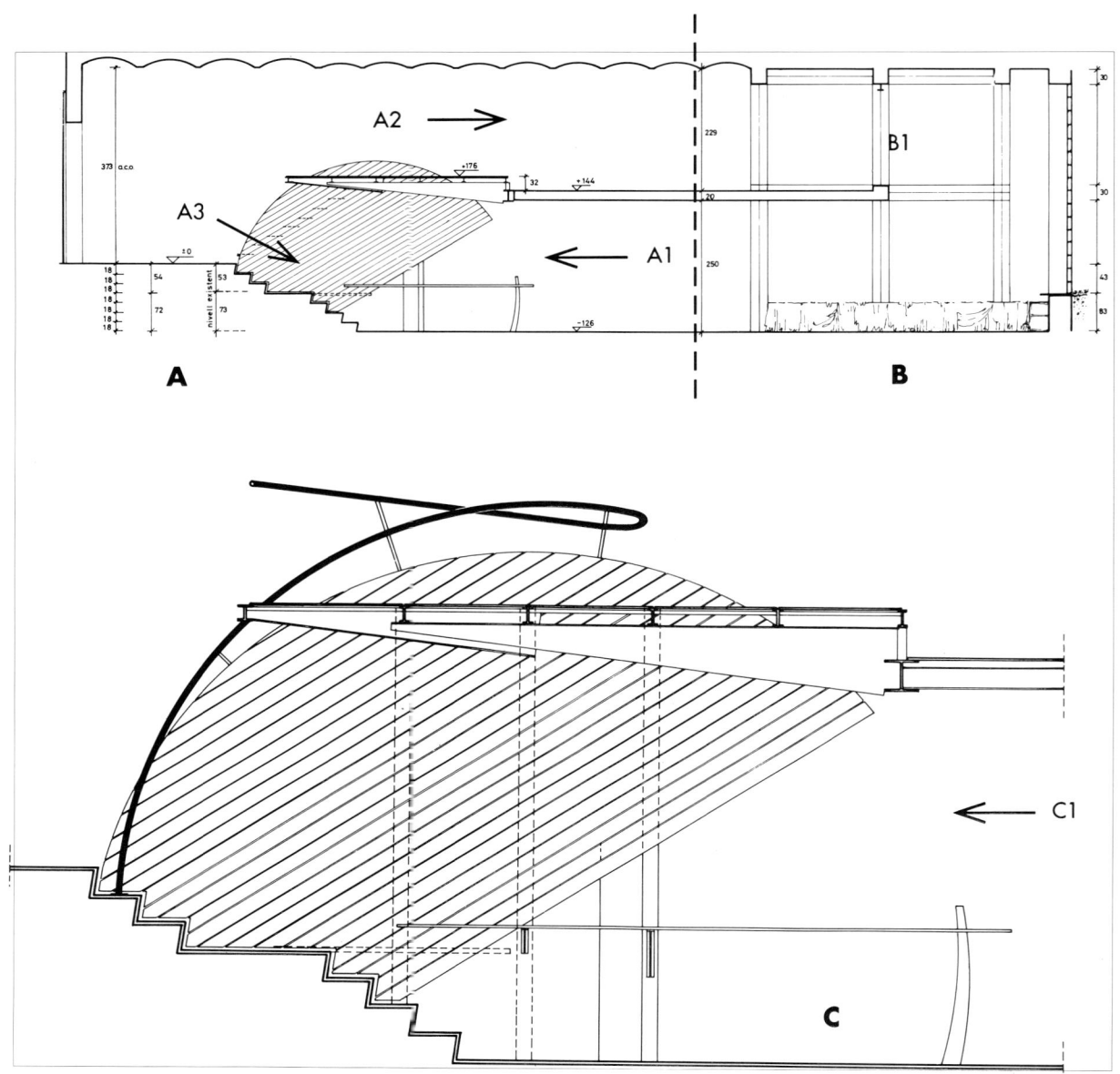

Section of the elevation of the premises. On the following page, view of the change in level between the two floors in the premises. (A1, C1)

Above, floor and elevation plans of the premises. Below, upper level of the shop, from where we can see the glazing at the entrance. (A2)

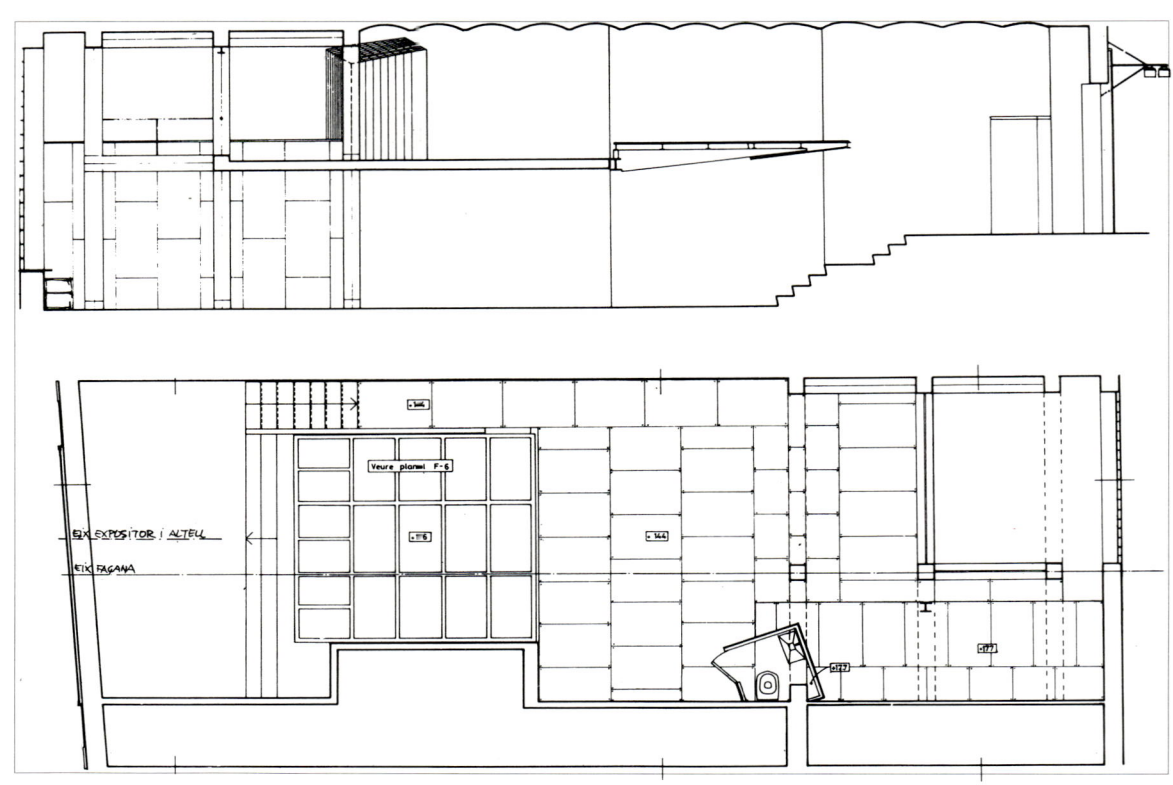

Perspective of the façade of the premises. (D1)

View from above the second level, intended as a display area.

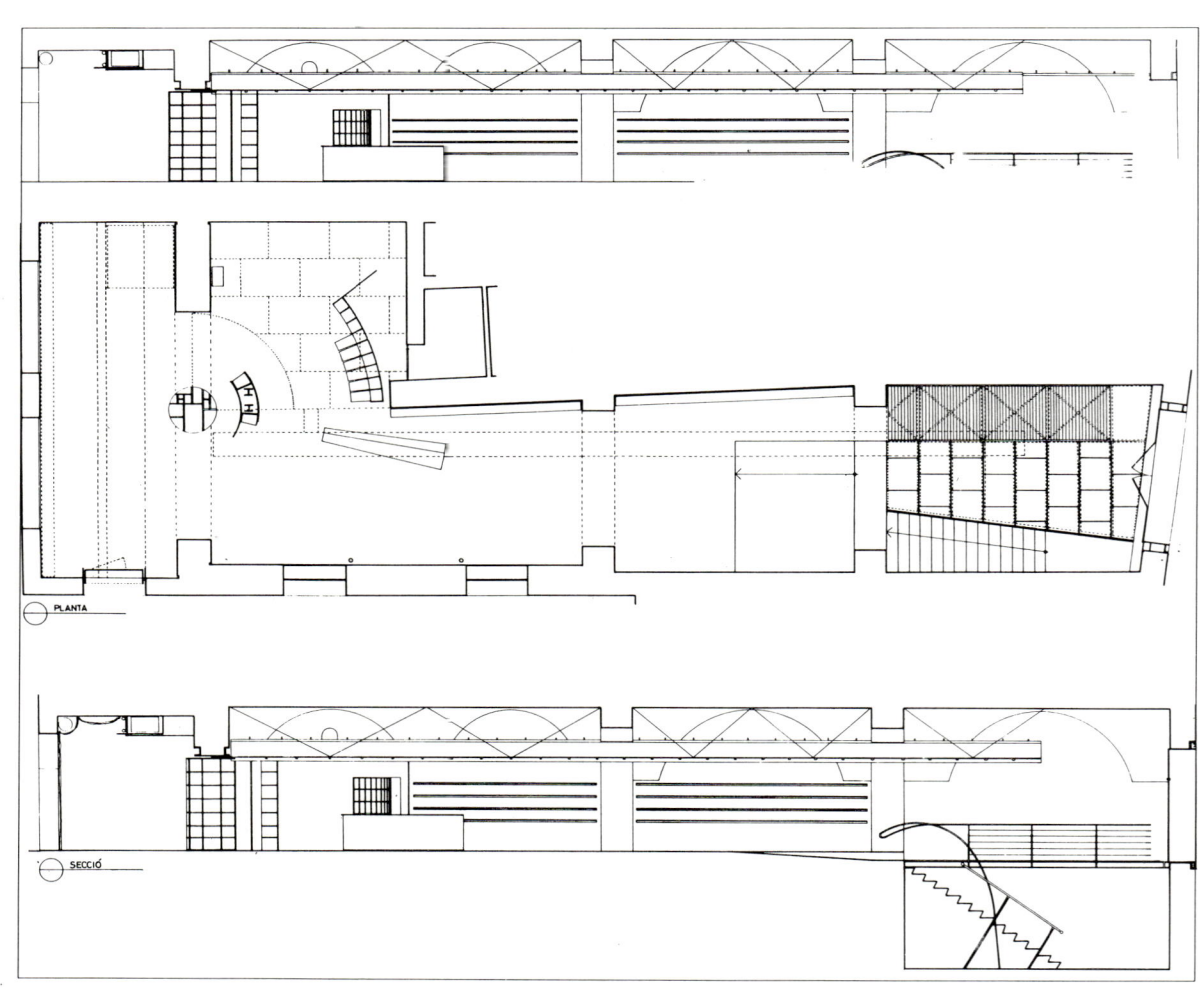

The originality of this project resides in the peculiar aesthetic form in which the initial objectives, marked out by the company, have been translated. The aim was to create a commercial network centred on shops, whose design was not seen as being as conditioned by sociological studies as are the majority. The aim was to offer a whole that was organised on the criteria of an internal identification, suited to the external reality of the urban nucleus, in which each of the shops would be located, without, that is, resorting to the use of reiterative and limited codes which often only create a series of cloned shops with little or no individual personality.

The initial project envisaged a programme for the realisation of a series of commercial

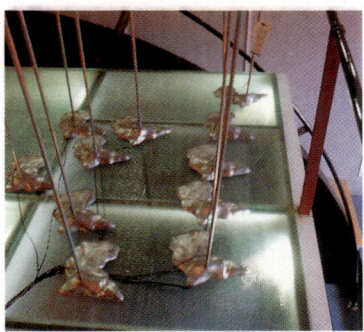

On the previous page, floor and elevation plans for the Addicional branch in the town of Banyoles, where we can appreciate that the structure and distribution are similar to the shop in Olot.

View of the second floor of the Banyoles premises.

On this page details of the entrance area of the shop, this time in Olot. (A, C)

Overall aspect of the second floor, view from the rear area of the shop (B1, D2) and plans of details of the display window, and part of the furnishings.

premises specialising in the sale of furniture and design objects, in different towns in Catalonia. The idea being to establish a criteria of identification which could be applicable to future branches. The intervention consisted of two lines of argument: first, the most functional, for the selection and organisation of products, and the other, with reference to the ambient image based on the treatment of the space, and its incidence in the urban background.

Starting out from these premises, the responsibility for the work was handed over to the prestigious studio of Pau, Martorell, Bohigas and Mackay, who are dedicated to architectural projects, interior design and the mounting of exhibitions.

In the Addicional shop in Olot, to begin with we found a very characteristic façade, marked by the presence of a frame which took in the entire entrance, establishing a species of formal dialogue with the historical tradition, as represented by Can Trincheria, where the shop is located. The glass of the display window is located on the interior plane of the wall, giving evidence of its thickness, and the cavities so typical of the XVII century. The luminous frame, and the black steel lining around the entire perimeter of the recess, support the typological characteristics of the original, but in turn perfectly frame the display of objects, giving it an image that is highly identifiable.

The architectural composition presents a division into two floors. The upper floor occupies the whole surface area of the premises, while the lower floor is only found below the light gantry.

The first is contemplated as a long visual sequence which runs the length of the floor until it reaches a wider area intended for display. This elongated structure is begun with a luminous frame, taking us into the passage, which is defined by arches supporting the roof of the structure, the mid-point of which provokes a formal compliment which gives way to an asymmetric effect of great visual force.

The second area, the wider area, has a series of openings which facilitate both the capacity for exhibition and the natural illumination. The difference in height is overcome by a metal stairway without structural supports.

The selection of products, in Addicional, is very important, and is centred on an ambiguous and eclectic offer which is materialised in historical and emblematic realisations, of an anonymous popular tradition, and the latest tendencies, this being led by the authors' own creations.

To summarise, the project for the chain of Addicional shops, using the premises in Olot as an example, are founded on a unifying proposal, based on a respect for the original urban architectural typology.

Access stairs to the lower level of the Addicional shop in Banyoles.

Rough sketch of the floor realised by the authors.

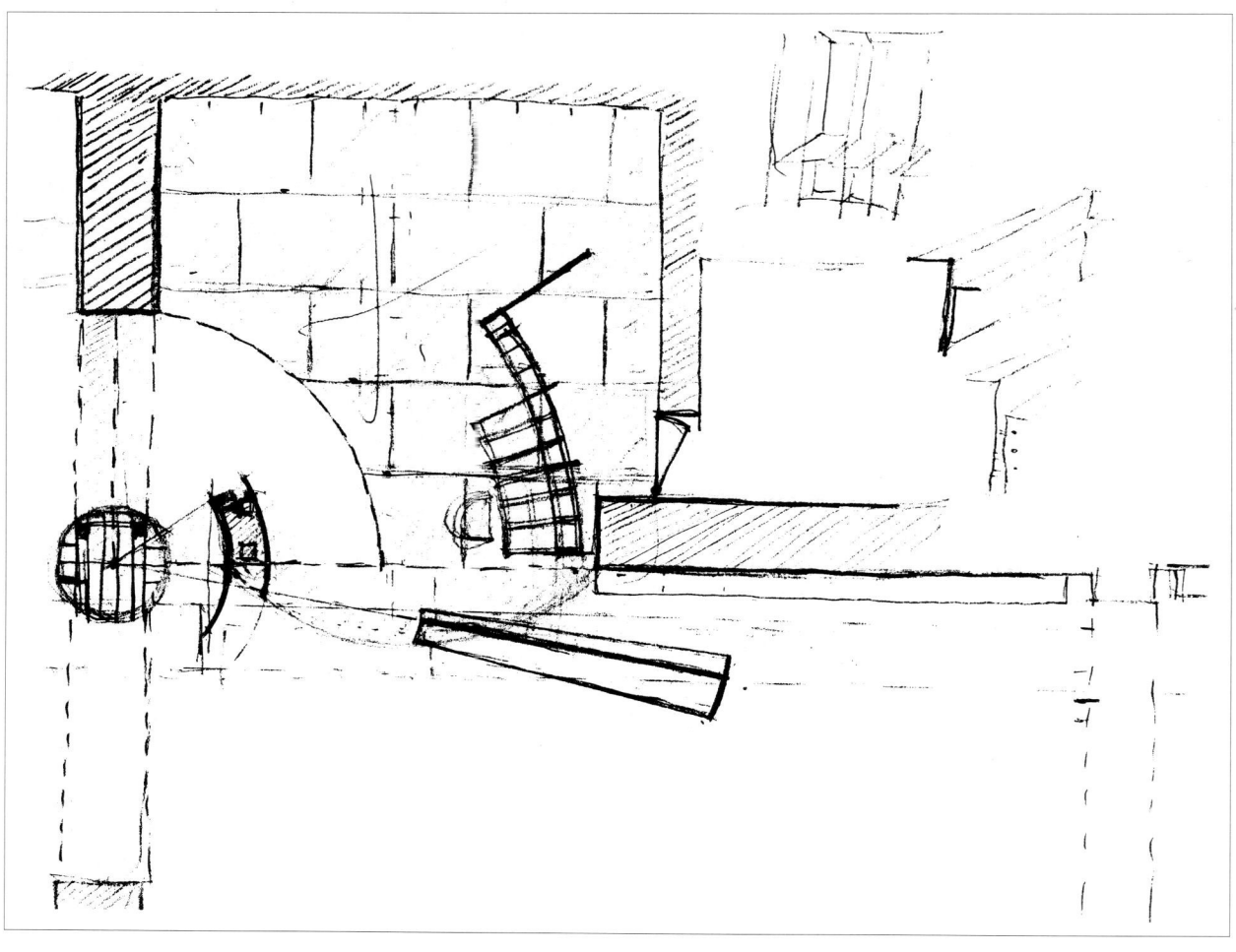

Details of the access stairs to the lower floor. (A3, D3)

Shoebaloo Shoeshop

Borek Sipek

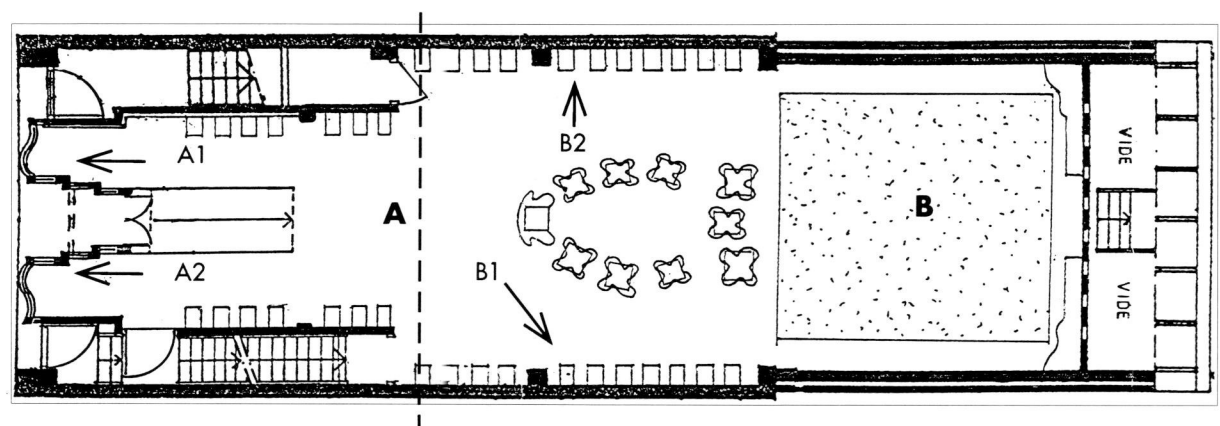

Floor plan of the premises.

On the following page, view of part of the display and sales area, where we can see some of the openings in the form of small mock windows, through which daylight enters. (B1)

Different aspects of the structural projections, converted into original displays for various models of shoes, and also the small counters distributed throughout the central area of the premises. (B2)

Shoebaloo Shoeshop, as well as being a footwear shop, is also a significative example of the creative tendencies of its author, the Czech Borek Sipek. The projection of representative scenarios, concerning the contradiction between present day man and the proposals of contemporary design, have led him to experiment with very personal combinations, of lines, volumes, planes and diverse materials. His aspiration is to enter, by way of design, into a conceptual dimension which goes much further than the mere comprehension of the visual.

Sipek became established as a designer in 1983, after some years working as a teacher of the theory of design, in the University of Essen. Since then, his work has been exhibited in the most prestigious artistic centres in the world. It is worth mentioning his honorific mention, in the 1983 edition of the German Architectural Prize, for his house of glass in Hamburg, that won the Kho Liang Design Prize, in 1988.

Shoebaloo Shoeshop was inaugurated in 1991, after Sipek's project was finalised, it was centred both on the remodelling of the lower part of the façade, and also in the design of the interior of the premises. The shop is to be found in one of the central streets of Amsterdam, occupying the ground floor of a neutral looking urban block of flats. In order to differentiate it from the greyness of the block, the author has surrounded the access door with a bright red sinuous structure, which acts as a delimiter of the space of the premises versus the exterior.

Original mirror, whose design is reminiscent of the shape of wings in movement, emphasised by a particular illumination based on spots. (B2)

A view of the display window from inside the shop. (A1)

The display windows are made up of a transparent glass laminate, bordered by a light coloured wooden frame, which profiles the structure and displays a few models of shoes. The form of the display is surprising: the shoes are literally hanging from orange coloured plastic tubes, inserted in small cylinders which are, in turn, inlaid in the lateral partition. The directional pull of the tubes, looking as if they wanted to break out of their containment, can be considered as a resource for attracting the attention of the passers-by and inviting them to enter the shop.

The interior is characterised by a rectangular floor of reduced dimensions, this being the reason for the elected disposition of the products, the design, and also the location of the furnishings, which attempt to transmit a spatial extension sufficient for a shop of this type.

One peculiar characteristic of the back wall of the premises is the placing of openings. In the middle and upper part of the wall small mock windows, which as well as their aesthetic purpose, serve to gently diffuse the outside light. The same wall serves as the support for an undulating masonry sill, the purpose of

Details of the multi-coloured relief frieze on the ceiling, and the structural projections and sills. (A, B)

which is the display of different models of shoes and bags; on the side walls projections are also incorporated to this display function.

The softness of the ochre and yellow tones of the walls, contrasts with the grey architecture of the building, and also with the bright red of the façade and the display windows. These smooth tonalities contribute to the creation of an intimate and cosy atmosphere, also favoured by the diffuse propagation of natural light, through the small mock windows.

The furnishings in the shop are characterised by a vegetable morphology, such as the contour of the display platform, in the shape of a flower, or the standard lamps which look like small trees. The mirrors are also framed by red metallic structures, which have the contour of wings in movement, their presence being highlighted by the placing of spots, which give them a special illumination, creating a play of light and shadow.

Shoebaloo Shoeshop could be considered as an "author's shop", given that we find here Sipek's most characteristic creative elements; undulating biomorphic adornments, small mock windows, or the form, which serves to

"decontextualise" some of the decorative components. However, its main merit lies in fitting the creative language to the functional needs of the project; creating a dramatic, and at the same time, a warm ambience, which channels the curiosity of the public towards the interior of the establishment. All of which, combined with the daring and functional display motifs, have resulted in a unique establishment, which is a reflection of the creative personality of its author. Projects like this one have led Borek Sipek to occupy a prominent place in the panorama of European interior design.

Another aspect of the shop display window, where we can appreciate the plastic tubes, used for hanging the shoes. (A2)

On the following page, different perspectives of the shop, where we can better appreciate the original design of the furnishings, particularly the displays. (B)

FOCHE MAINA

Manuel Ybargüengoitia & Maria del Mar Nogués

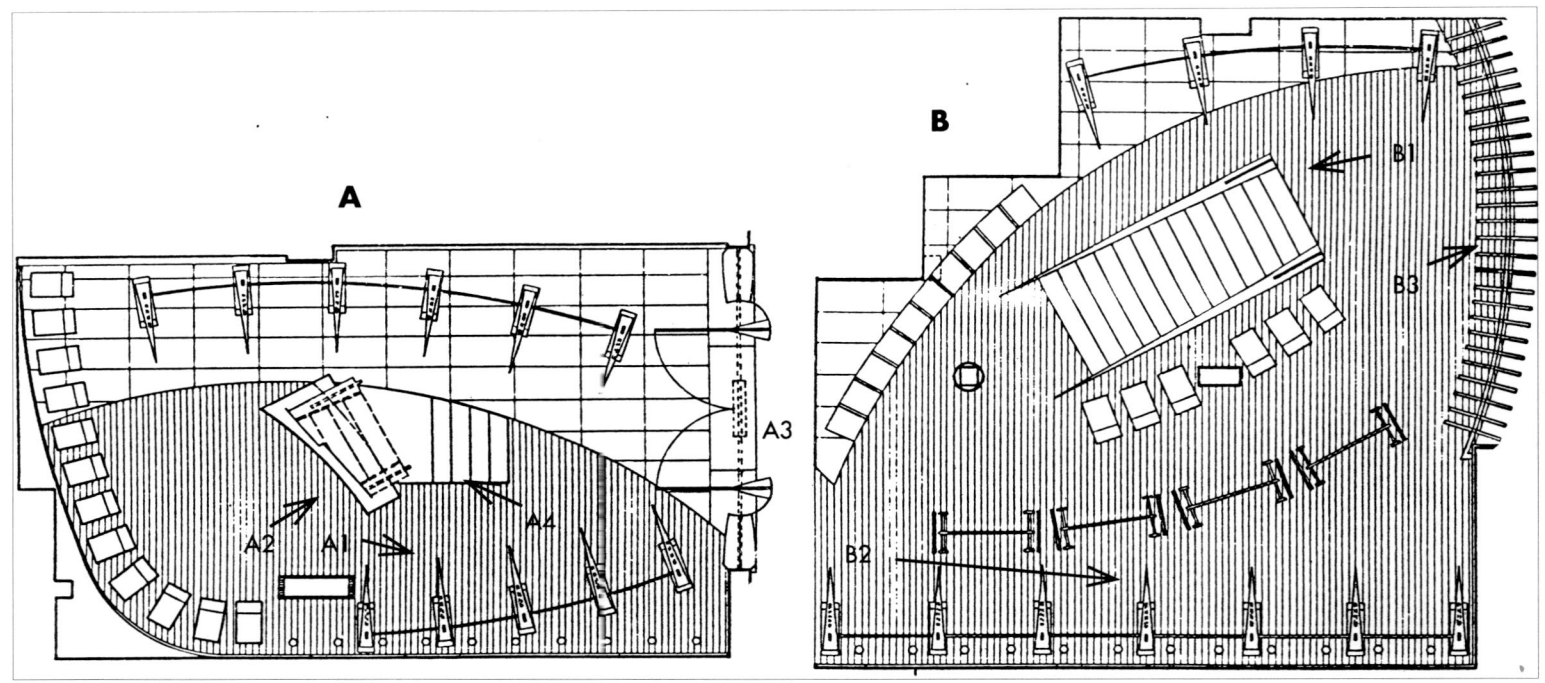

Floor plans of the premises.

Overall image of the second floor, with Foche Maina's anagram in the background, and the original displays at the sides. (B1)

Decorative elements, of a great expressive force, one of the characteristic notes of the premises. (A1)

On the following page, the main counter, under the stairs, completely realised in wood. (A2)

The achievement of the work of these two interior designers, in the Foche Maina shop in Barcelona, is in expounding schemes which question the conventional precepts of display windows and façades, in order to benefit a suitable connection between the interior and the exterior. The expressive intensity of the company's anagram, and the large perimeter clothes racks, in the shape of an osseous structure, reveal the subordination of the architecture to the functional programme. The uniformity of the ambience is achieved through the use of a series of recurrent materials; copper, bronze and wood; through the semantic weight of the furnishings; and through the communicating structures (the large main staircase) and the display structures.

The work of Ybargüengoitia and Nogués is, preferably, centred on the realisation of overall projects, and in the industrial design of diverse objects. From their collaboration a series of works of diverse functionality, which are deserving of attention, have come into being, all of them in Barcelona; the shoe shop Eleven, The Pool "de Comunicación" offices, the restaurant Ticktacktoe, the boutique Sinequanone, and the Tombbús line of buses, among many others.

The initial objective of the project which concerns us here, consisted in the remodelling of old premises, so as to convert them into a men's clothing wholesale shop, for the brand name Foche Maina. The premises are located in a building of Barcelona's Ensanche district, with a surface area of some 160 m², distribut-

Plans of the displays on the second floor. (B2)

The company's anagram and an emblematic image, cut out of sheet copper and methacrylate. The intense blue colour converts this figure into the centre of attention, due to the chromatic and material contrast with the rest of the decor. (A3)

Detail drawing of the display units.

ed over two spaces on different levels. The renovation process was based on a complete stripping down of the premises, this being its indispensable point of departure, on the basis of which, the structural and formal distribution of the interior would then be possible.

The space is organised on the basis of a plurality of components which are matched and contrasted in order to furnish the new design with a certain expressive force. These elements are arranged so as to mark out a natural interior cadence.

The surface area is set out on two floors, connected by a singular stairway, which also serves to distribute the sales space which surrounds it, and which constitutes one of the functional and aesthetic axes of the shop.

The contents of the shop are displayed in their entirety by means of an open façade, a subtle combination of solid and fragile components joined together in harmonious fusion. The doors have an oval shape, and are finished in cast copper, giving them a design of chromatic beauty. The attraction of the façade rests in the suggestion of lightness and transparency, with a visual contribution based on the use of glass and copper, which serves as an inducement and as a symbol.

The total perception of the interior and the display window concept, free of glass case separators, gives an idea of width and the fullest use of the display areas.

The aesthetics of the premises are dominated by the great perimeter clothes racks, and also by some distinctive wooden shelves,

On the previous page, plans of the second floor of the shop. (B)
Above, original directional spots, placed over the shelves which can be seen in the photo below. (A)

where the products are arranged. A great prismatic column supports the first floor support beam. The hangers become wrapping elements, the authors intention on creating them being to evoke the skeleton of a dinosaur, limiting and defining the space at the same time as it creates its own cadence.

The Foche Maina project was definitively organised through a series of elements with a high expressive and semantic content, which left the architecture of the premises as a backdrop. These components redefine and distribute the space in a way which is more decisive than that achieved by the walls and partitions. The conjunction of stairs and hangers, as well as the overall concept of the interior, based on an open façade, determine the spatial organisation of the premises.

Ybargüengoitia and Nogués manage, in this way, to offer the image of premises that are distanced from the conventional precepts, but which pay special attention to an aesthetic that is both attractive and suggestive, and which is fast becoming one of the main characteristics of young Spanish design.

Above, an overall plan of the stairs which communicate both levels. Below, plan of the narrow and curved form of the clothes hanger area, realised in wood and copper. (A4)

Display units on the second floor, executed in the same materials, wood and copper, predominant in all of the decoration of the premises. (B3)

Shu Uemura

J.L. Veret & G. Ronzatti, of Atelier des Ouvriers Reunis

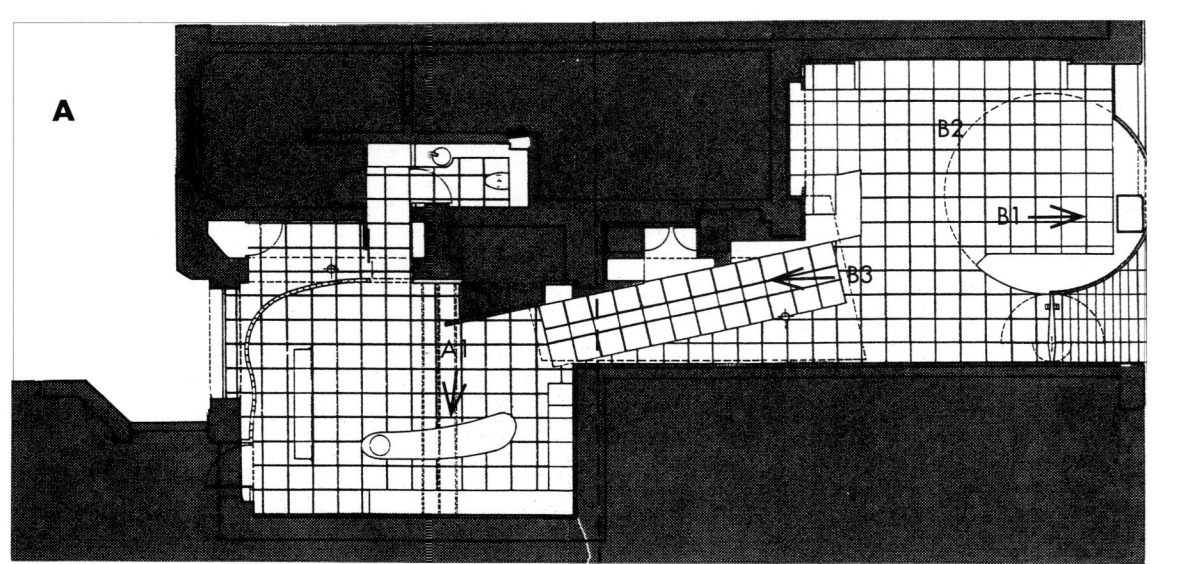

Floor plan of the premises.

Following page, aspect of an area of the display window. (B1)

The Paris branch, of Shu Uemura, the international chain of perfumeries and cosmetic centres, is in the heart of the St. Germain-des-Prés quarter, a traditional haunt of artists and creative people.

The shop has been conceived within an avant guard context, according to the spirit of the man who inspired it, the great Japanese make-up artist Shu Uemura. The integration of the space that the shop occupies in the quarter takes precedence over the decoration and the design, this being inevitably subject to fashion, that in itself, is becoming increasingly more ephemeral.

The visual impact of the façade is achieved by means of display windows, built into a cylindrical glass and wood structure, the top of which shows off the shop sign, illuminated by large spots, set out in a circle surrounding it. On the entrance door another sign, vertical this time, emphasises the character of the space, marking out a certain conceptual distance from the traditional perfumery; not only are there sales, but also consultancy and advice on the art of beauty.

The premises contain two differentiated spaces, linked by a passage. In the first room make-up items are exhibited, on a rectangular glass slab table, separated from the display window by a low dais.

As a prolongation of this dais there is a granite slab, affixed to the wall and which, together with the great long mirror which is also affixed to the wall, constitutes the visual testing area. The white laminated wall and the granite of the flooring harmonise with the light coloured wood, creating an apt framework for the display and demonstration of beauty products.

In the display window samples, and those on show in the interior, there is an evident pre-

Different detail drawings of the shop, both from the outside and the inside.

Following page, aspect of the large glass display table and part of the area of the entrance. (B2)

Previous page, above, view of the passage which communicates the two areas of the shop, with the display shelves (B3), and below, area at the back of the premises. (A1)

On this page, aspect of the wall and the mirror, for make-up tests. (B3)

dominance of make-up products, above all on the shelves, which run the length of the left hand side of the premises.

On the right there is an irregular display structure, of light coloured wood, placed against the wall, and divided into various volumes. Moving along the passage, we come to a room, where a superior metallic structure supports spots and light projectors, giving the area a scenographic character. A wooden counter in the form of an irregular ellipse displays different ranges of products on metallic trays.

The space is comprehensively conceived, according to those criteria of function and harmony, designated for the greatest possible promotion, of what is essentially the main aim, the sales, complemented by consultancy on matters of aesthetics and beauty. All of which is impregnated with that balanced and conceptual spirit of interior design, which traditionally holds sway in the commercial premises of Japanese companies, whether or not these are realised by the Japanese themselves.

LORCA CRAFT CENTRE

Juan Antonio Molina

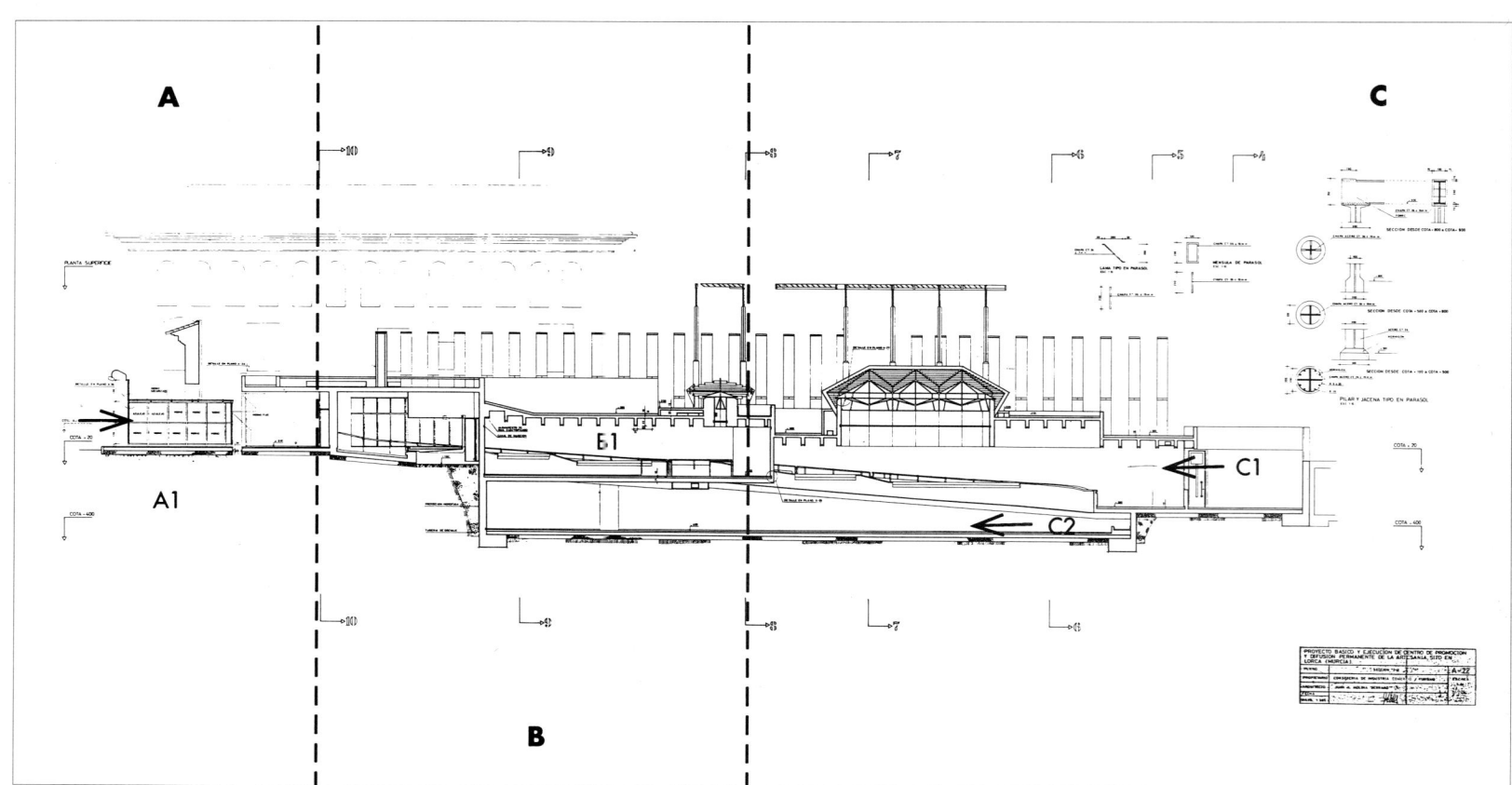

Elevation plan of the premises.

Panoramic view of the principal exhibition area, where the distribution and communication function of the ramps, and the glazed roofs can be appreciated. (C1)

Partial aspect of one of the exhibition areas, at the lower level of the site and a detail drawing of the same. (C2)

In the photo below, view of the communicating passage including the start of the main ramp. (B1)

The following page, general view of the end of the ramp, after it has run for a length of over 50 metres, and aspect of the main exhibition rooms. (C1)

Below, the entrance to the Lorca Craft Centre. (A1)

The Lorca Craft Centre is situated in the very heart of the city, in a building of atypical structural characteristics. The author, Juan Antonio Molina, is currently working, from his studio in Murcia, on a whole range of architectural projects, both on buildings and on installations of a more ephemeral character. Before he came to dedicate himself totally to his work as an architect, he was closely involved in educational activities, as a teacher in the Murcia School of Applied Arts and Artistic Trades, as a speaker, and also as a collaborator in various of the communications media.

The craft centre occupies a predominantly elongated space, with a gently sloping ramp of over 50 metres in length, running the length

of the space. At the back of the premises there is a platform, from which another similar ramp runs down in the opposite direction towards an exhibition area, some six metres down. Between these two ramps intermediate spaces are created, which are used for the exhibition of pieces and objects.

The principal area of the space is located at the end of the longer ramp, which is where the reception, the lavatories, the meeting area and a lecture hall are found. Here we also find an alternative exit, the goods entrance, the installation switch cupboard, etc.

Under the main entrance more reduced spaces are found; for audio-visual projections, craft demonstrations, and various exhibition rooms.

An isolated staircase connects the different levels, offering a quick communicating route between them all, although the intention is that normal circulation in the premises will follow the route laid out by the ramps.

The lighting is based on a combination of halogen directional spots and natural light, which comes from the glazed roof. This combination of effects creates an all embracing atmosphere, which is full of nuances, endowing the main space with an air which is both warm and suggestive.

Definitively an original solution for a space with a difficult structure and configuration, which has been advantageously resolved in order to achieve large exhibition areas, coherently communicated, without ever losing sight of the aesthetic and artistic criteria.

Malls

Commercial and Hotel Centre in Hamm

Brigitte & Christoph Parade

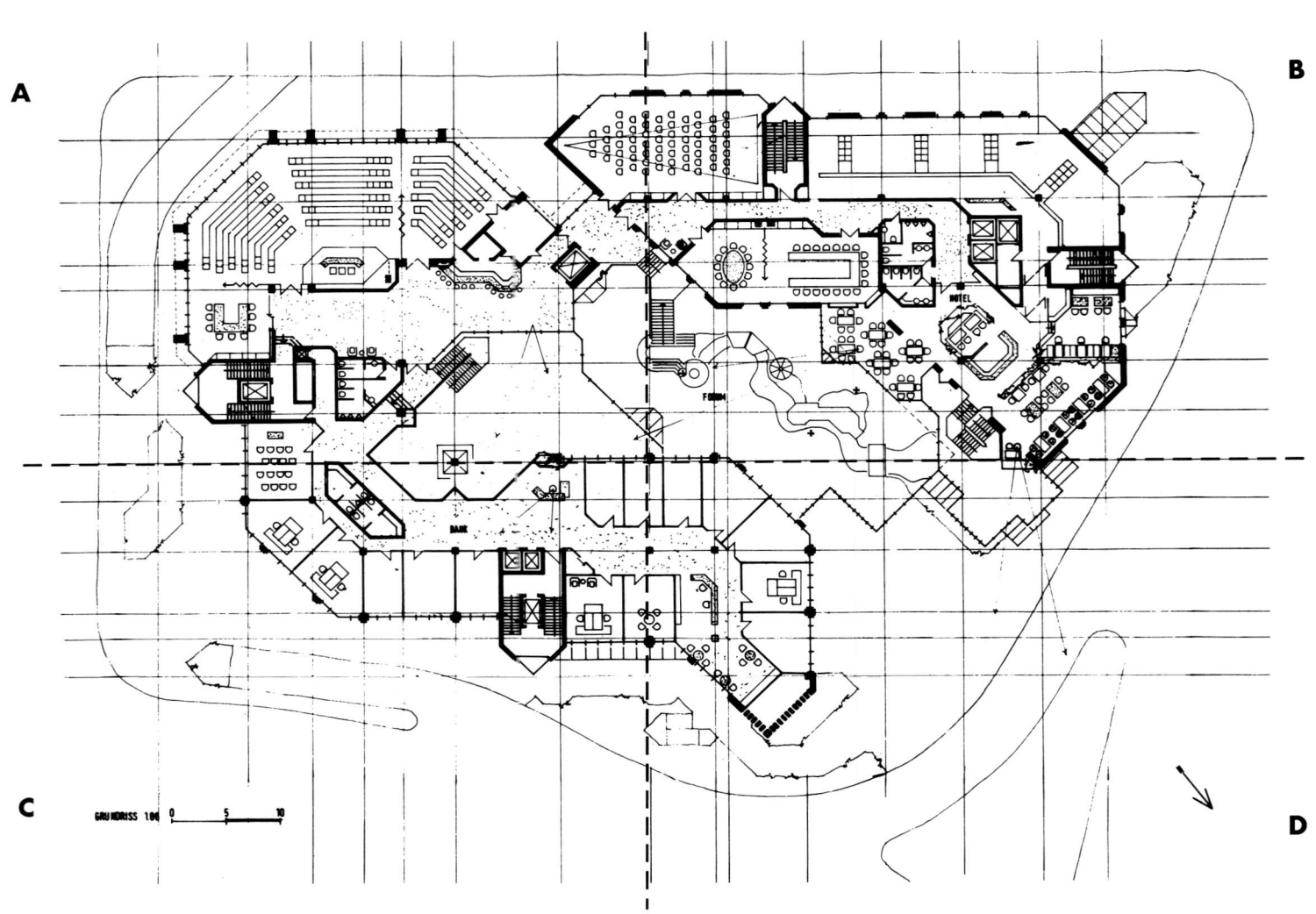

Floor plan of the whole area of the complex, with detailed distribution of the different areas.

"Elevation of the complex"

"Access to the building"

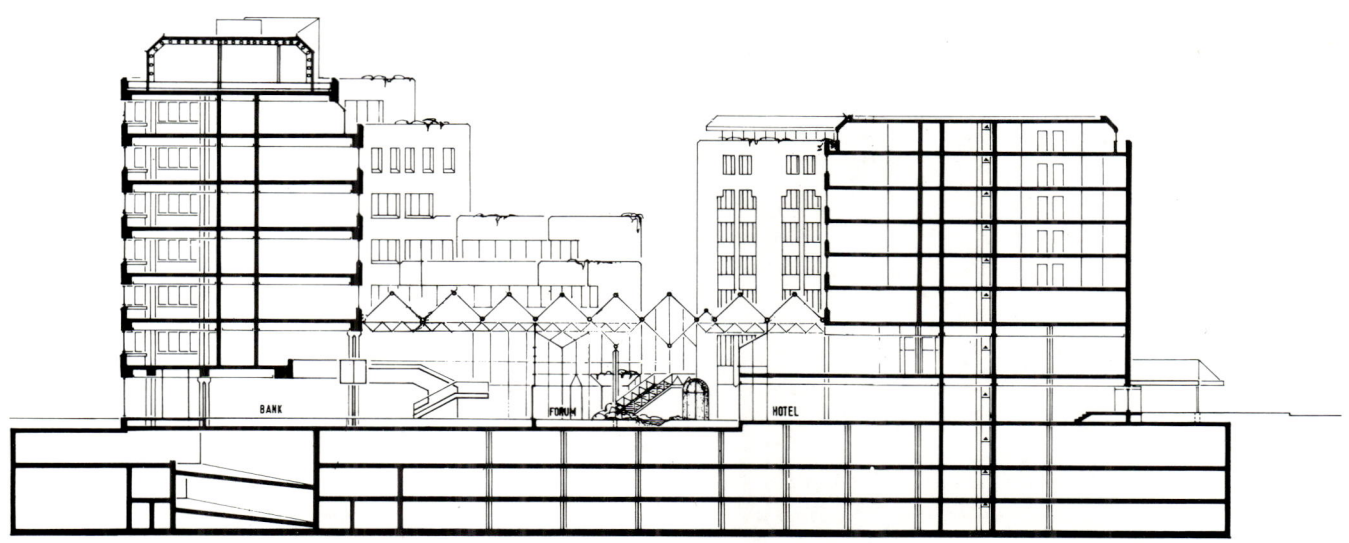

An aspect of the accesstairs to the second level, and in the photo below, the main information counter in one of the entrance halls. (B)

The project which we present in continuation is the fruit of the joint work of two German architects, united both professionally and also personally. Brigitte and Christoph Parade studied architecture at the University of Stuttgart, and completed their training in Vienna and the United States respectively. Since 1962, the year in which their professional association began, they have been awarded more than 120 prizes for their work; notably for the Hückelhoven Civic Centre, the Gladbeck Communications Centre, The German school in Rome and the Museum of Natural Sciences in Osnabrück.

For the construction of this commercial centre in the German town of Hamm, a competition was held in which the criteria for selection was the election of the project which would best give form to the promoters' desire to endow the town with an authentic nucleus for its economic life. The space had to house the head office of the bank which financed the project, a large hotel and a whole variety of shops. The fact is that the original idea was for a multi-storey building, whose silhouette would bestride the urban landscape, and which would have a garden area opposite.

Another aspect of the exterior of the complex, the central sector.

In response to this outline the architects presented the project which finally saw the light of day, a project which was very different from the promoters' original idea, but which ended up convincing everyone. It is based on the creation of a space which attracts the public for the quality of life created around it.

For this purpose two buildings of a normal height were provided, one for bank offices and the other for the hotel, communicated by a comprehensive covered space in the form of a pedestrian precinct, with a restaurant, a cafe and shops. The area to be internally organised like a small town, characterised by the diversity of spaces, forms and structures. A diversity which can be observed in every part

In the above photo, section of the floor where we can appreciate the height distribution of the building. (B)

Detail drawing of the lamps located throughout the interior area. In the photo below, a plan of the exterior of the building, with its original metallic structure, and its glass roof.

Detail of the interior of the cafeteria.

of this multi-centre, from the bank's central lobby, to the hotel's interiors, where variety and originality are the predominant notes.

The attempt is made to create a sensation, in the visitor, of desirable and lasting well being not only through the commercial spaces themselves, but also through the "landscape" of the interior area, completely glazed, surrounded by prismatic arcades, whose aesthetic quality combines futuristic elements with rocks, plants, fountains and strategically placed points of light. The mixture of traditional materials (for example exposed brickwork) with modern metallic structures is also of great interest.

If we add to this the extra attraction of the sunlight, which floods in through the glazed roofing structure, bringing with it a warm and cosy ambience, we have a suggestive background which transmits the quality of life that was the initial intention of the authors, and which has clearly been fully achieved.

On the following page, the overall plan of the bank's main lobby. (C)

Stockholm Södra

DOM-Borowski

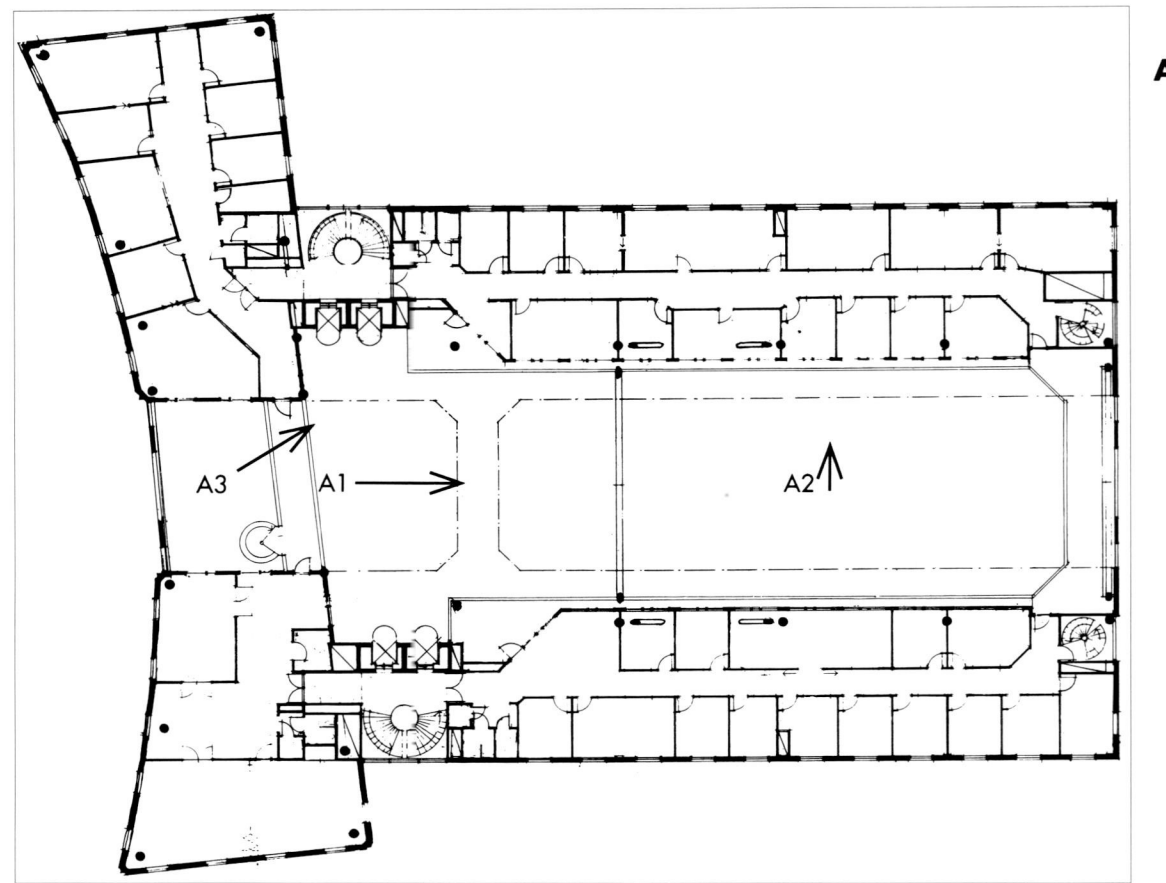

Floor plan of Building. (A)

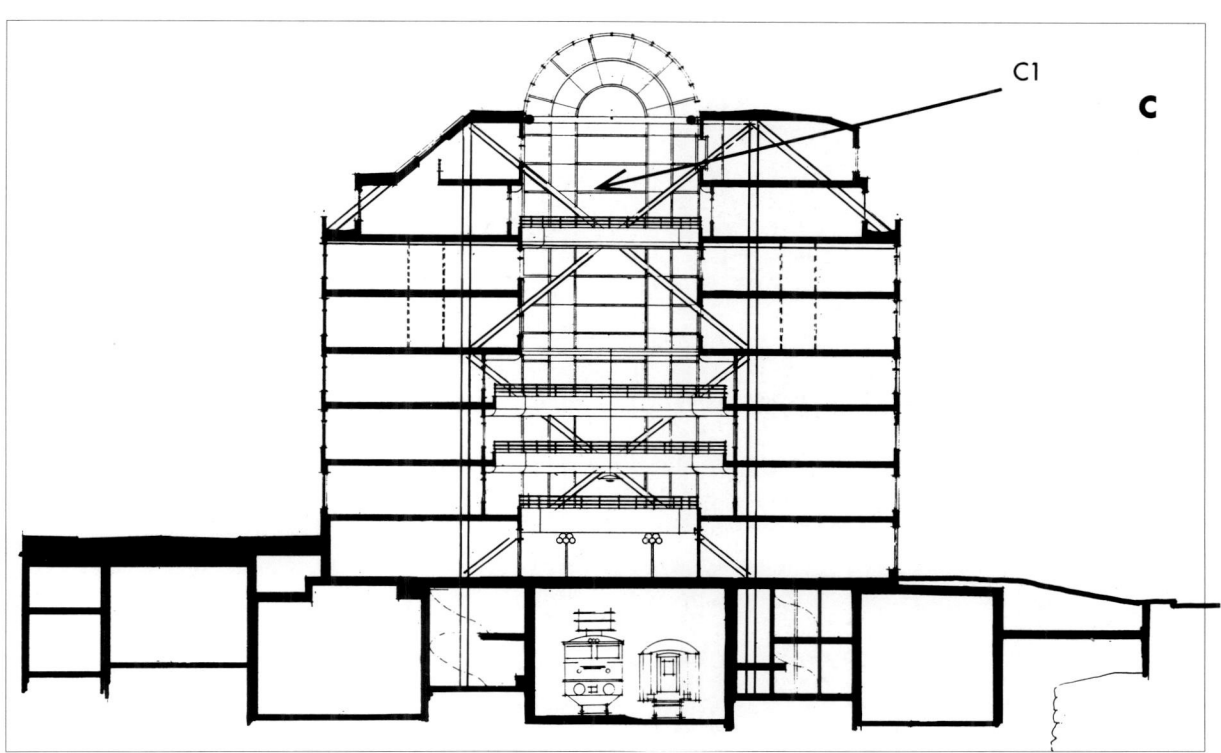

Plan of façade. (C)

The Stockholm Södra building, realised by the DOM-Borowski Arkitekter AB studio, in the Swedish capital, is an exemplary instance of the new concepts for public spaces, characterised by the possibility of multiple uses; by the taking advantage of natural illumination; and by a free and natural circulation inside the space. To these criteria the authors have incorporated a series of stylistic and aesthetic elements which give the complex a tremendous capacity of expression, based on formal audacity and the use of innovative construction techniques.

DOM-Borowski Arkitekter AB consists of a group of 50 professionals, led by the Pole Mischa Borowki and the Swede Krister Akeby. They generally realise projects for the construction of new residential buildings and offices, and above all, they are involved in urban planning and interior design. Their international projection is outstanding, with works realised throughout the continent of Europe.

We find the origins of the Stockholm Södra in an urban development plan for housing and commercial spaces in the centre of Stockholm, in an area built around the railway station in

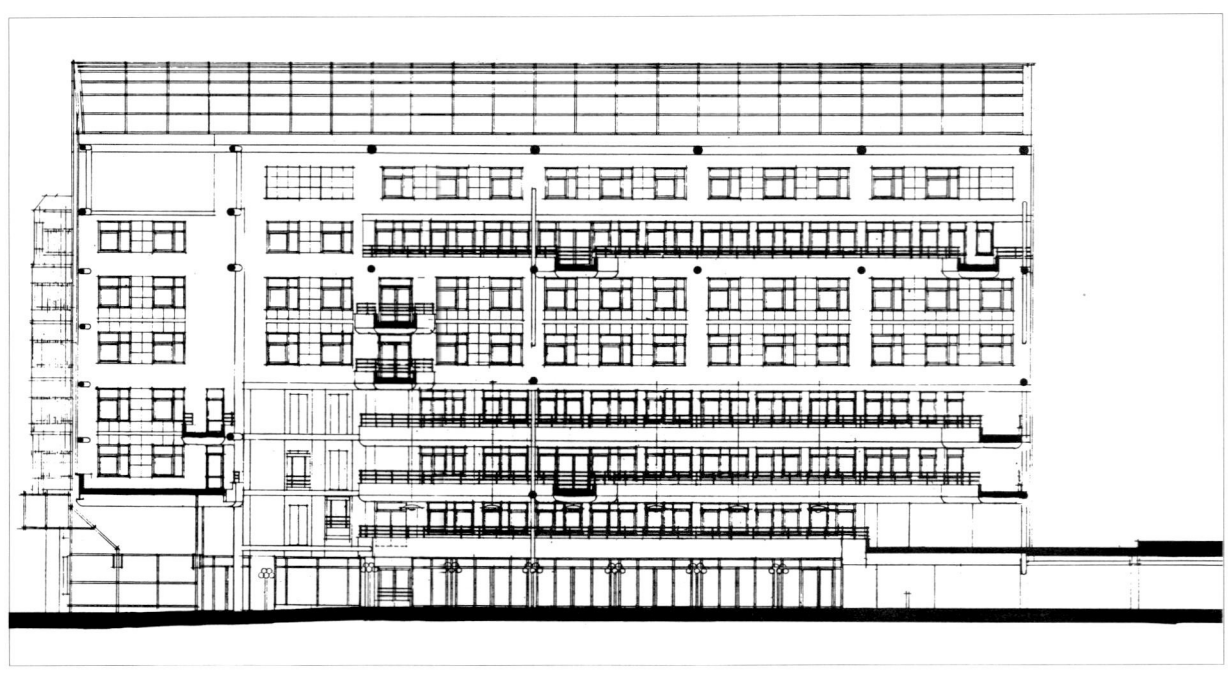

Transversal section of the internal structure. (C)

the south of the city. The future building would have to be the means of access to the underground rail system.

As well as this principal function, the introduction of other utilities, related to the current criteria for public construction, was proposed, especially areas for offices and commercial establishments. For this reason the work was structured according to the most up to date and innovative architectural and interior design tendencies, with the aim of givingthe whole an air of practical, and at the same time aesthetic modernity.

The inconvenience of maintaining the operational activities of the rail traffic during the construction period – from 1988 to 1990 – was resolved by means of a an external retaining structure, which avoided the transmission of pressures to the ground. This constructive strategy, in great part, decided the volumetric configuration of the building, based on two parallel bodies related by means of a glazed central space, which would be the aesthetic and functional nucleus of the project.

The glazing process leaves exposed the supporting structure, mentioned above, consisting of black steel tubes, which intersect in

Detail of the façade. (B)

On the following page, perspective of the interior of the central sector, where the great metallic retaining structure and the glazed roofing, which covers the whole area, can be appreciated. (A1)

the air above along with the bridges connecting the two blocks at a variety of levels.

The main façade is an element of great architectural interest, both for the expressive contrast of transparency and opacity, between curves and straight lines, and also for its capacity to adapt to the urban background which envelops it.

In the interior atrium, the importance rests in the clear and transparent ambience which floods down from the roofing, and also in the achievement of a fit space for the movements and circulation of the public.

In the aspect of the use of materials and colour, the project is based on the contrast between transparent components, such as glass, and others which are more opaque,

such as the metallic retaining structure. In order to give relevance to the latter, an intense black has been used which stands out amidst the overall whiteness and clarity of the interior. The railings and the steel structures of the shops have an intense blue tone, while the area of the atrium and the galleries have been floored using a combination of limestone with white marble hues.

In conclusion, all of these skilfully combined elements, both architectural and aesthetic, constitute this multi-space, which represents a perfect example of the new tendencies in the design of public spaces, adapted to an urban background.

On the previous page, view from below, of the great metallic structure which surrounds the building. (A2)

In the above photo, the difference in height between the two lateral modules and the central sector can be appreciated, and also the contrast between the flat and the domed covering. We can also see the transparent clock which overlooks the upper part of the building. (C1)

On the previous page, different perspectives of the supporting metallic structure.

View of the three galleries which surround the entire perimeter of the central area. (A3)

COLLIER CAMPBELL

Michael Brown, Stephen Ibbotson & Anthony Charnley

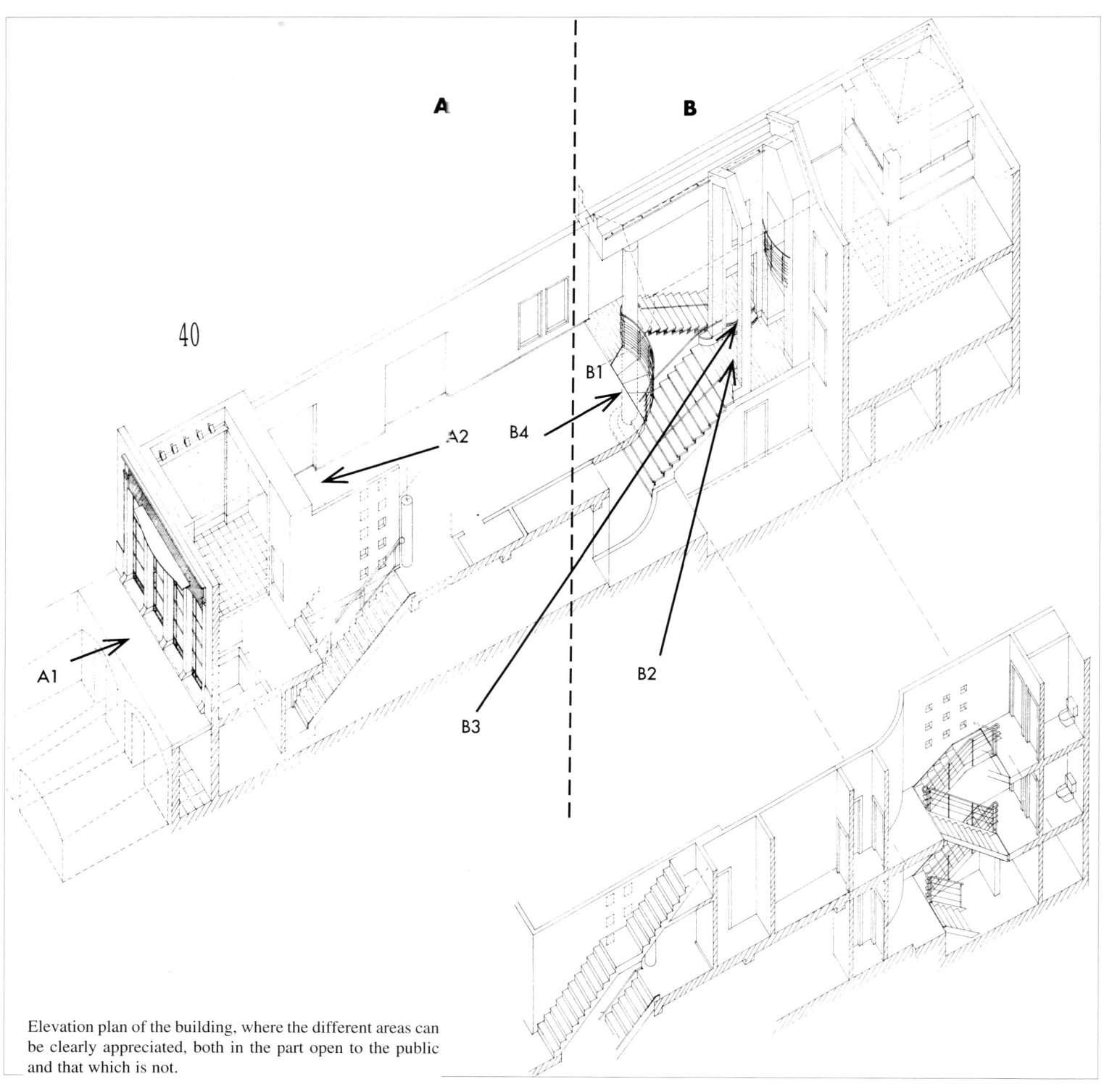

Elevation plan of the building, where the different areas can be clearly appreciated, both in the part open to the public and that which is not.

Façade of the establishment, and below, decorative detail of the entrance to the shop. (A1)

Sara Campbell and Susan Collier are two recognised English Stylists who had not, until a few years ago, established themselves on their own account. In 1987 they decided to create their own trade mark and to inform the public at large about their projects. For this purpose they took over an old building in the Mayfair district of London, which had to be refurbished in order for it to become a commercial centre.

The restructuring was handed over to Brown, Ibbotson and Charnley. These three architects, after prestigious individual careers, decided to become associated in 1985, forming the Brown Ibbotson Partnership. Among other projects they have realised the restoration of St. John's Church, the Little London Court and Van Hage's Garden Centre.

The original building was located in an area of Georgian dwellings, occupying a rectangular space which stretched back endlessly from a narrow façade. The configuration of the floor plan was less than ideal for a commercial establishment; among other things the circulation through the interior was difficult, due to the presence of a labyrinth of walls and a warren of stairways. All of this would have to change radically.

Perspective of one part of the first floor and of the main stairways. (B1)

The reform had to be directed towards the possibility of exploiting the elongated floor plan and the narrow façade, and also to a strengthening of the sensation of verticality. This was achieved by means of the incorporation of a plexiglass roof which stimulated the perception of the establishment as a unitary whole, and also allowed for the diffusion of natural light from the top of the premises, down to the wide stairs of the hall.

In order to mark off the distinct sales points (materials, clothing, furniture, ceramics and crafts) plaster partition walls were used.

The vertical projection of the staircase has been emphasised by a sort of tower which has been erected around it, with an open frame set out frontally in reference to the entrance.

The result is a flexible and open space, with a spatial amplitude, obtained by the elimination of useless barriers and the abundance of natural light filtering down from the glass roof. The restless and untiring character of the designers is reflected in the dynamism emanating from the interior of the premises.

After the remodelling, the distribution was the following: the access floor, dedicated to fashion and accessories; the area of the main stairway for the display of fabrics, which were draped from the banisters, unfurling down to the ground floor. At the back of the shop there is a bed linen display, the basement harbours

Another aspect of the first floor where the plexiglass roof, which allows a diaphanous natural illumination during the day, can be appreciated. (B)

Distribution area for the main stairways (B2), and above, detail of the metallic banisters. (B)

the materials and furniture section, and the lower floor, at the back, is reserved for a store and offices.

From the access area the customer can see the curvilinear balcony, from which the vividly coloured fabric samples are draped, contrasting with the consciously neutral white colour of the walls.

In the area set aside for fashion is the desire to create a typically English atmosphere, based on antique furniture combined with pieces from the twenties and the white ceramic tiles, which have been omnipresent in the urban decoration of the British capital, since the last century.

As to the materials used, the authors have opted for solidity and durability: plaster walls, pine and American oak floors, slate for the exterior façade, and the flooring in the entrance,

On the previous page, a magnificent perspective of the building at its full height, withone of the two curvilinear balconies overlooking the entrance, and the fabrics, a splash of colour against the whiteness of the walls against which they hang. (B3)

View of the windows which give onto the façade from the interior balconies. (A2)

and oak laminate refurbishing for the steps of the main stairway.

For the lighting a combination of small low voltage tungsten spots and coloured fluorescent bars was used.

In this project nothing has been left to chance and the result is an intermediate solution, somewhere between a personalised atmosphere, reflecting the character of the designers, and a suitable public space; both for the products which are on display, and for the kind of customer that is expected. The sobriety of the architectural and decorative resources contrasts with the variety of forms and the chromatic richness of the fabrics and objects, combining to form a balance which is both pleasant and cosy.

The same perspective, as on the previous page, this time with the area entirely decorated and lit. (A2)

Detail drawing of the decoration in this same area. (A)

Following page, overall plan of the central atrium and its glazed roof. (B4)

Showroom Cassina Japan

Mario Bellini

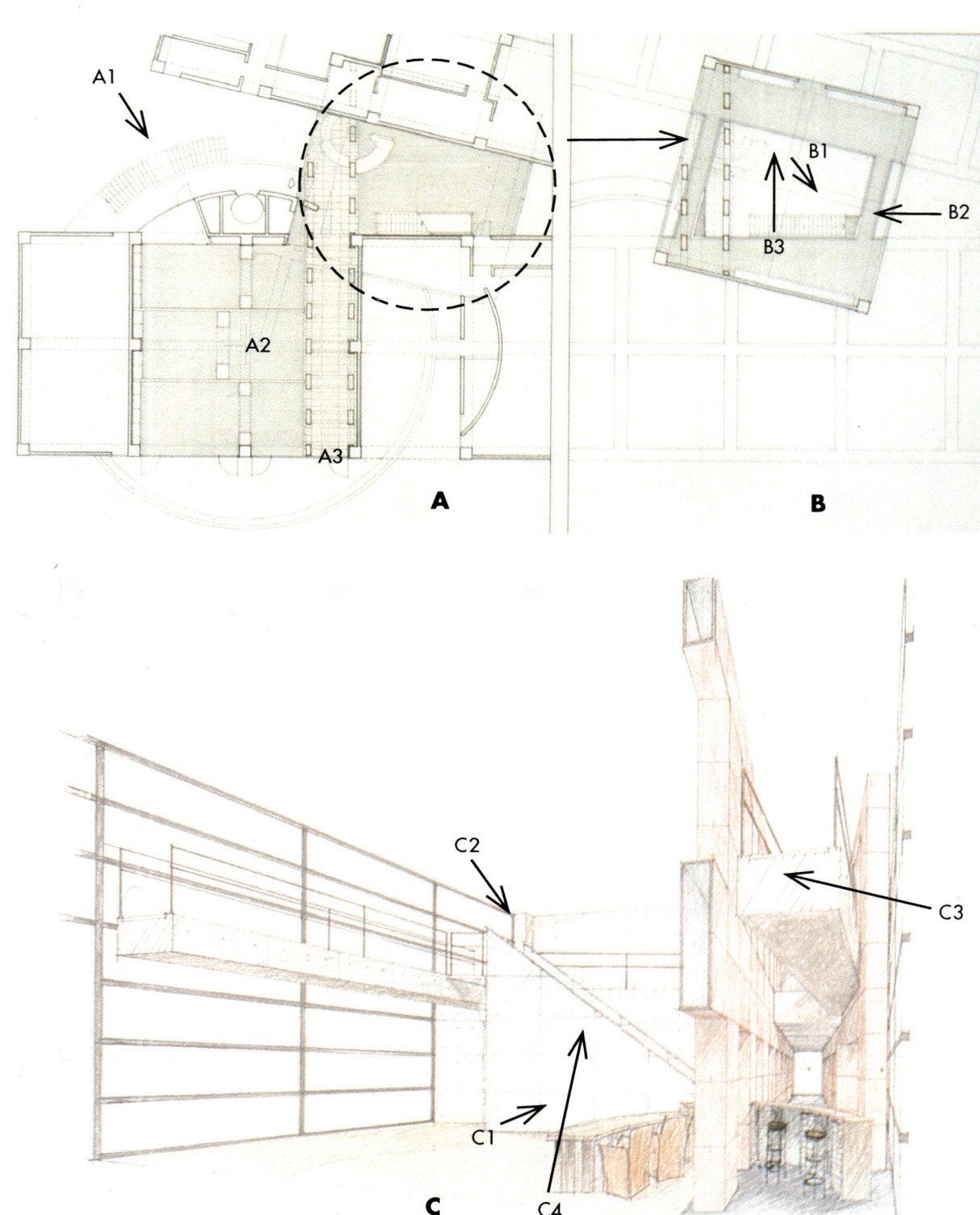

The professional work of the Italian architect Mario Bellini has often been centred on projects in Japan, these being realised for either European or Japanese companies. One of these projects has been the creation of a showroom, for the Italian furniture design company Cassina Japan, in Tokyo.

This project has been based on the design for a commercial exhibition space, which harmonically reflects Japanese creative values alongside Mediterranean cultural elements. The purpose of this relationship is to demonstrate to the public the coming together of the company's origins, and its mission to expand in the land of the Rising Sun.

Born in Milan in 1959, Mario Bellini, among many other activities, has taught, and has participated in conferences and in seminars organised by prestigious universities and cultural centres, such as the Domus Academy in Milan, UCLA in Los Angeles and the Architectural League in New York. His work has been internationally recognised with the award of numerous prizes, twenty-five of his projects are included in the New York Museum of Modern Art's Permanent Design Collection, which dedicated a monographic exhibition to him in 1987.

Floor plans of the two levels of the premises, and section of the elevation of the ground floor.

On the following page, panoramic view of part of the periferic gallery and of the first floor access stairway. (B1, C1)

On this page and the following page, exterior view of the premises, in the highest part of the building conceived by Tadao Ando. (A1)

Above, view of part of the ground floor, from the top of the stairs. (B2, C2)

In the photo below, the exhibition area, on the highest floor of the premises. (A2)

Following page, different perspectives of the perimeter gallery. (C3, A3)

Bellini has worked for such companies as Olivetti, Vitra, Rosenthal and Yamaha, not forgetting his enduring professional relationship with Japan. He has been invited, together with other prestigious architects of international standing, to participate in the competition for the design and reorganisation of Berlin, as the capital of a unified Germany, an initiative which was promoted by the German Museum of Architecture, the Frankfurter Allgemeine Zeitung and the Berlin City Council.

The premises of the Cassina Showroom in Tokyo, a project finished in 1989, are located on the upper floor of a building by the great Japanese architect Tadao Ando, which also houses many shops of Italian origin, such as Krizia, Verry, Uomo and Gianni Versace; making the contents of this building an authentic Italian stronghold within the difficult commercial universe of Japan.

From the outside the premises have the appearance of a perfect cube, of a double height, with overall glass covering. Three basic areas can be differentiated, two for exhibition and one for communication, the latter, due to its aesthetic importance, has become the fundamental axis of the interior design.

The first exhibition area has one floor in the shape of a quadrilateral inscribed within a circle. It is surrounded by a double height interior gallery, marked off with glass covering on the two side walls, while the other walls are cement constructions. This space is the neurological centre of the exhibition area due to the clarity which results from the glazing. The dou-

ble height allowed for the incorporation of perimeter exhibition areas which favour the idea of a natural sweep and increase the capacity of the space for the exhibition of their products.

To gain access to the upper perimeter levels, Bellini introduced a highly effective structural element, both functional and expressive;

On this page, new perspective of the gallery, from the second level. (A3)

The following page; above panoramic view of the outside of the building, from where the internal structure of the space can be appreciated, overlooked by the gallery which joins the two floors. (A1)

Below, view of the premises from the ground floor, with the entrance area in the background. (B3)

a metallic and lineally designed stairway, affixed to one of the walls, a piece with an almost sculptural quality, having a notable impact on the sober aesthetic of the premises.

The second exhibition area, with a trapezoid floor is of more reduced dimensions; the ceiling is lower, corresponding to a single level. The interior-exterior relationship is maintained, in this section by means of a terrace, which opens out onto the street through a glass panelled wall. The luminosity originating from this terrace is taken advantage of, so as to leave the space completely empty, handing the maximum protagonism over to transparency, and the items of furniture being exhibited. Pieces from the company Cassina share the space with items of classical design, among which names such as Le Corbusier, Tobia, Scarpa, Reitveld, or Bellini himself, are highlighted.

The new Cassina Showroom in Tokyo is, then, the result of a harmonic and creative marriage of Japanese and Mediterranean elements. The character of this intervention is reflected, for example, in the relationship which is established between content and container; the building designed by the maestro Tadao Ando, geometric, abstract and lyrical, in the most pure Japanese tradition, lives in perfect harmony with an interior based on architectural and artistic elements, clearly reminiscent of the Mediterranean, offering us a fine example of aesthetic harmony between Orient and Occident.

BOUTIQUES

The Thierry Mugler Boutique

Patrick Philippi

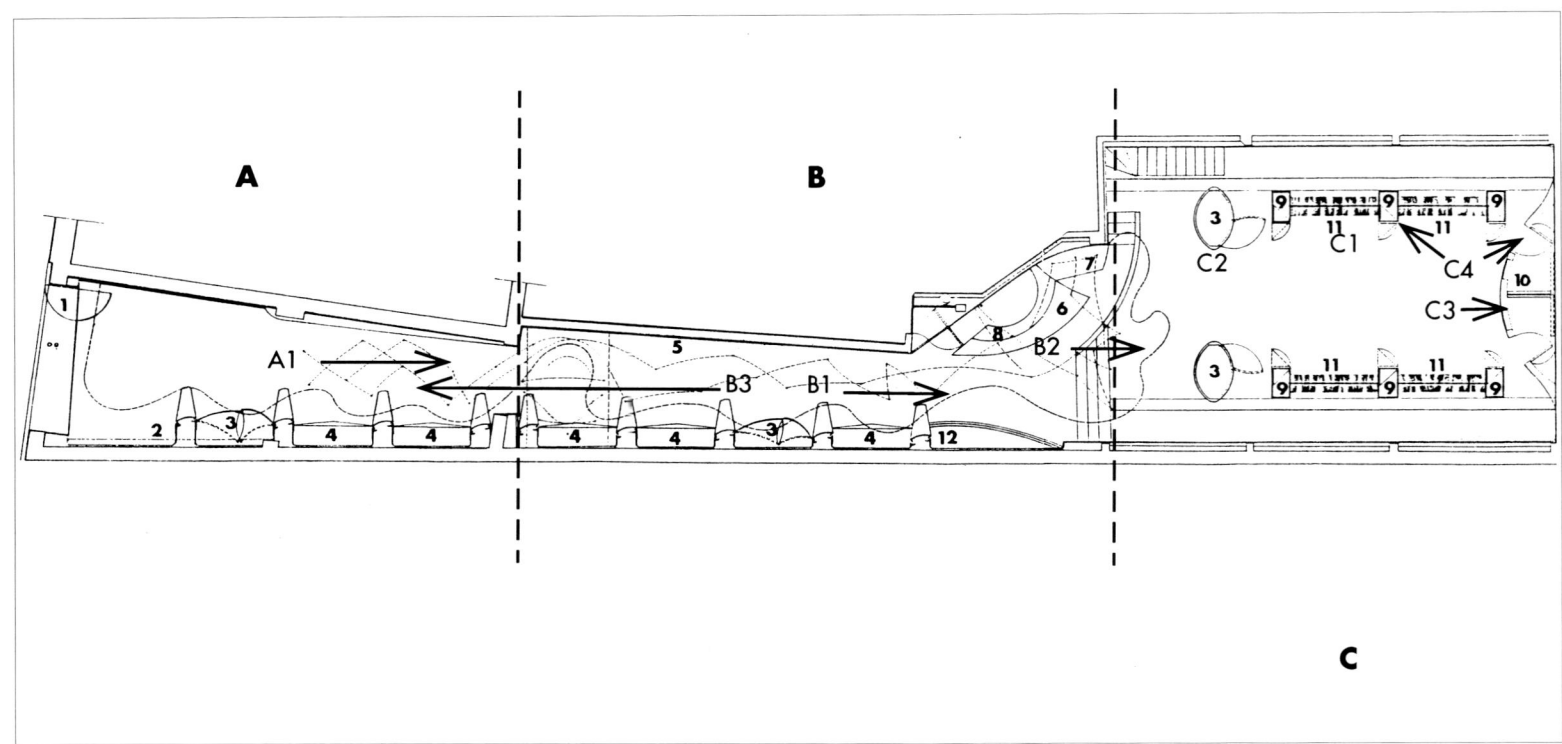

Floor plan of the premises, with the distribution of the various areas.

Within the most creative tendencies, concerning commercial spaces, mention must be made of the success of the "boutiques"; sales spaces showing the latest novelties of a company, or a designer, along with their classic products. That triumph has been influenced by numerous factors, standing out among them is the power with which present day society endows the ephemeral dictates of fashion. This type of project is an interesting reflection of the present cultural and economic situation of the West.

An example of a women's clothing "boutique" can be found in Paris, in the shop which the designer Thierry Mugler has in he very heart of the capital of fashion. It is the work of the French architect Patrick Philippi; born 1940, he has worked on numerous projects, both architectural exteriors and also interiors. Among his most recent work we should include the plans for the Strasbourg Museum of Modern Art, in collaboration with Arata Isozaki, and for the Polytechnic School of Strasbourg, together with Oswald M. Ungers, which are worthy of note.

All of the Thierry Mugler shops, including the Paris branch, bring us into contact with a supernatural ambience, dreamlike expressionism, characteristic traits of the creations of Thierry Mugler, which are reflected in the architecture and interior design of the commercial premises.

The shop, which has no display window, is separated from the street by an invisible non-reflecting glass which attracts the curiosity of

Perspective of the long corridor which runs across the establishment. (A1)

Plan of one of the shelving units, for articles of clothing. (C1)

External aspect of one of the fitting rooms, of an aluminium structure and with theatrical lighting. (C2)

On the following page, partial plan of the passage, with the shelves for mens clothing. (B1)

the passers-by, as a result of the architecture before the fashion. The somewhat unusual composition of volume, a long corridor which traverses the premises, determines a very compact space. The play of forms inspired in elements such as air and water, and combining different tones of blue, and light that is intense when it is focused on a mannequin and subdued on the changes in level, and the corners of the premises, contributing to the creation of an innate universe, reflecting the personality of the company's trade mark.

The whole establishment is treated as an enclosure, with walls and ceilings realised in papier-mâché, following free forms and painted in matte blue. The floor covering, made up of a directly poured mixture of marble, stone and tinted resin, allowing for a complete liberty of forms and colours, which combine on the floors throughout the premises, and on the stairways. This system has also been used on the horizontal surfaces.

This unreal ambience is fostered by an indirect illumination, projected onto the curves of the ceiling, or onto the furnishings, and then directly lighting an occasional point, such as the mannequins. The greater part of the light-

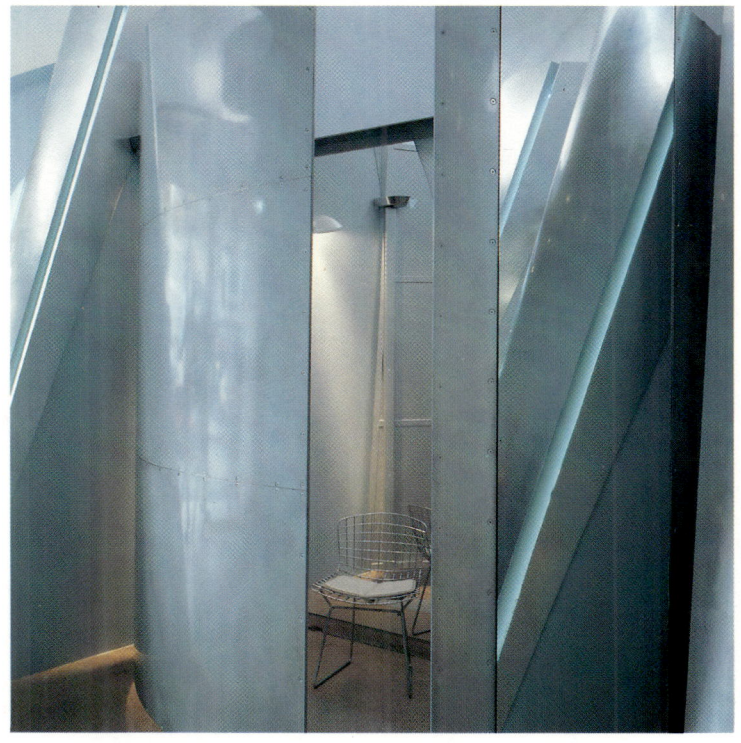

On the previous page, access to the ladies fashion space, whose mannequins appear to be inviting us to enter. (B2)

Another aspect of one of the fitting cubicles. (C3)

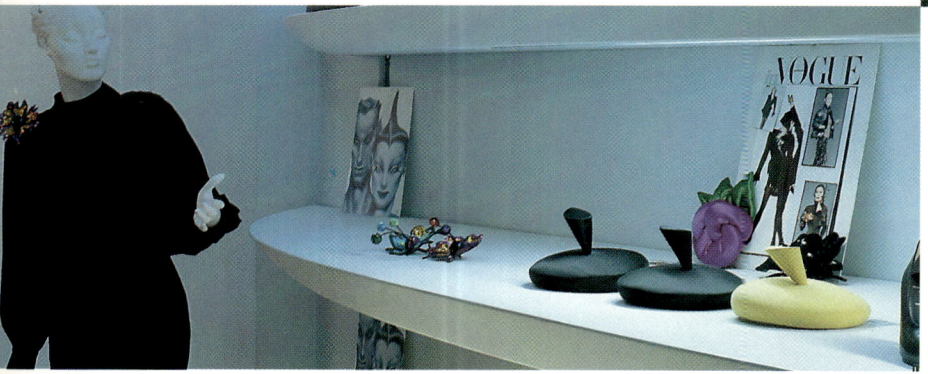

A view of the long passage, where the sinuous soffit (plan of detail) can be clearly seen, realised on the ceiling, which hides the installed system of indirect lighting. (A1)

In the photo below, a detail of the clothes racks where the products are presented. (C)

Interior and exterior of the double fitting cubicle, located at the back of the shop. (C3)

Right hand side of the ladies fashion area, with a single fitting cubicle, and a large mirror. The semi-unreal ambience is realised by the combination of indirect light, projected onto the roof, and direct light on the bare concrete points, such as is the case with this fitting cubicle. (C4)

Aspect of the interior of the shop, and on the right, a plan of the passage from the interior, where it can be appreciated how it is the architecture that is emphasised more than the clothing on display. (A, B3)

ing consists of coloured neon and fluorescent tubes, coated with a film of tinted gelatine.

This contrasts with the back of the shop, where skylights shed a natural light, which does not alter the original colours of the clothing.

At the end we find the fitting rooms, realised with painted aluminium panels, lit from top to bottom, using a theatrical technique.

With a view to the changes in the market the organisation of the space is completely modular, the different elements being transformable and interchangeable. The annexes to the premises are fitted out to allow for possible extensions.

As we can see, the idea of realising a project which could be adapted to future fluctuations and demands has been considered from the very beginning and is, up to a certain point, logical, dealing as it does with a commercial space whose very "raison d'être" is rooted in a concept as changeable as fashion.

Issey Miyake

David Chipperfield Architects

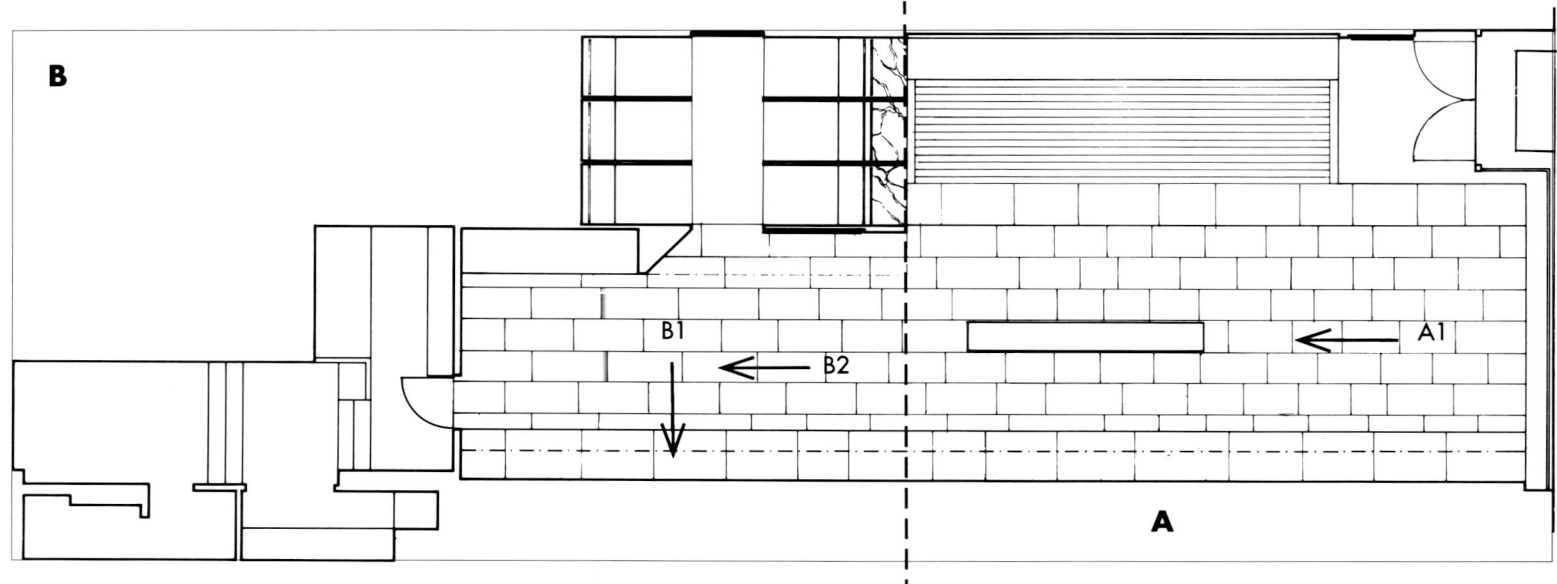

Floor plan of the premises and their distribution.

In the upper photo, view of the lower part of the shop, where the straight lines and the geometries are predominant. (A1)

In the lower photo, illuminated display window, which seeks to underline the conjunction between design, quality and prestige. (A2)

In the very centre of London we find the shop of the Japanese designer Issey Miyake, a project based on old commercial premises, which had previously been dedicated to the sale of Japanese clothing articles, and which were completely remodelled, from the point of view of aesthetic concepts.

The responsibility for the project was given to the interior design and architecture studios of David Chipperfield Architects, founded in 1984 by a young avant guard group, who do, however, possess an excellent professional record, specialising in interior design and projects for projects as individually distinct as restaurants, private buildings, museums, commercial premises, etc.

Since the days of the original old premises a series of substantial changes in the manner of understanding the nature of exportable fashion has been produced, on the part of Japanese businessmen. From a commercial business, dealing in traditional fashion and stocked with easily exportable cliches, it has gone on to become a totally different concept, based on traditional elements which are inseparable from Japanese millennial cultural, yet adapted to current reality, principally that of

the great modern cities of Japan, and of the rest of the world.

A philosophy based on austerity impregnates the forms of the Miyake shop in London, a reflection of the simplicity and characteristic clarity of the architecture of Japanese interiors. Form and content are indissoluble, and not only fashion is sold here, but also a specific way of understanding the fashion, and by extension, many other facets of human existence.

The display window and the access to the premises are integrated into a glass partition, which does not, however, contain any of the articles of clothing that are sold inside the shop, but instead displays an original abstract figure as the principal element of decoration. The intention here is that the shop premises themselves should be displayed from the entrance, balanced, austere and completely removed from conventional designs which are based on graphics and pictorial elements.

The Chipperfield studios understood straight away this manner of interpreting commercial spaces, and employed, in this project, the greatest possible simplicity of line, as far as possible, setting the clothing aside and

Abstract design figure which constitutes the only decoration in the display window, which in this way overcomes its function of display, and acquires symbolic connotations. (A2)

Simplicity and clarity become excuses for the creation of real and unreal spaces, in which the articles of clothing have an importance based, not only on their form and colouring, but also on their textures and qualities. (B1)

strengthening the internal universe of the shop, in a reference more to the spirit than to the image.

This was translated in the construction of previously nonexistent dimensions through elementary materials, such as wood, marble or stoneware, in such a way that the elements and the disposition of the whole succeed in living together, without strident contrasts, in a harmony which makes easy the dialogue between past and present.

Overall plan (photo above) and more closed (photo below) of the area at the back of the shop, with two fitting rooms and the counter as the main elements. (B2)

EKSEPTION

Eduard Samsó

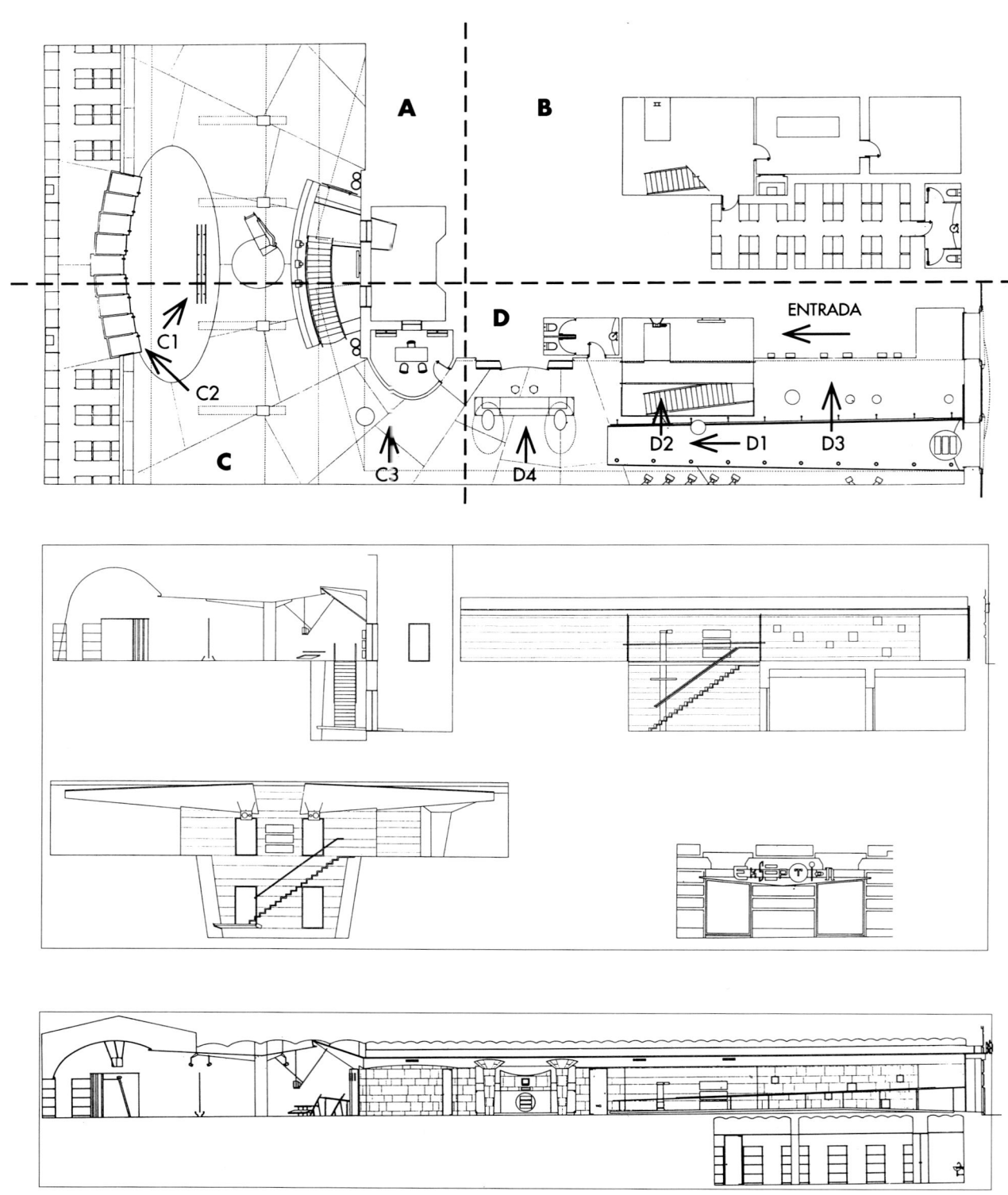

Outstanding within the world of emergent Spanish design, characterised by its passion, fantasy and decorative ingeniousness, is the figure of the Barcelonés Eduard Samsó, who has established a fine international reputation for himself, thanks to the serious, personal and honest trajectory which he has maintained.

This young architect, born in 1956, started his professional career in 1980, merging industrial design, interior decorating and architecture. His work and his exhibitions have frequently been awarded prizes, he has been a finalist for the FAD and the Delta prizes on numerous occasions. He has managed to combine his professional activity with educational work in the Eina School in Barcelona, and as a speaker and participant in radio and television debates. Public recognition of his work is reflected in the profusion of his exhibitions and in the frequency with which his projects appear published in the specialised international media.

With the project for the Ekseption shop in Madrid, the conception and understanding of space had to predominate over and above the elements of interior design. The author resolved this by means of a devaluation of conventional concepts, such as the display window or the main entrance door, converted by him into a continuous sequence communicating, without any physical barrier, the exte-

In the foreground, plan view of the premises, both of the main area and the store area. In the following, different sections of the elevation of the premises, both longitudinal and transversal.

Perspective of the long corridor which communicates the entrance area with the display and sales area, where details can be appreciated of the suggestive illumination used. (D1)

In the photo below, the stairs to the basement, which is used as the store. (D2)

rior of the premises with its heart. The concept of the interior as a natural sweep converts movement, space and light into essential components of the establishment, over and above the other stylistic elements.

The shop has no display window facing onto the street and no entrance door; the only protection is that of a slightly undulating awning, supporting the metallic anagram of the company.

On this basis the physical connection between the two ambiences of the premises is set forth. The solution is presented in the form of a slightly convex carpeted walkway, which draws people off the street, and almost without them realising it, leads them into the very centre of the shop.

On both sides of the long passage two areas are set out. The left hand side, practically built into the wall, is characterised by a series of graded spots which project their light towards the floor, as if to dramatize the moment of entry. The right hand side fulfils, to a certain degree, the function of a display window: a metal sheathed wall, housing recessed cupboards with wooden interiors, displaying those clothes which are most representative of the company.

The encounter between the reception area and the centre of the shop presents a set of

Next to the store access stairs, is the walkway which connects the long corridor to the main area of the shop. (D2)

In the lower photo the system of illumination can be clearly appreciated, based on strings of halogen spots. (C1)

On the previous page, overall plan of the fitting rooms area. (C2)

On this page, some of the details of the decoration can be seen, dominated by the metallic surfaces. (D3)

perspectives and perceptions of the spatial volume of the premises. The interior of the central nave does not present any division, everything is in view, and as a result the shop assumes its function on the basis of its own structure. The space is ordered without the need to establish limits or separations; the surface is open to any use and allows for any lay-out. With this strategy the moulding of the space to the demands of the product is achieved, and not the other way round, as usually occurs in conventional commercial premises.

The fitting cubicles receive an almost architectural treatment, with an urbanistic lay-out in the form of small blocks grouped together. Above them there is a great simulated celestial vault, the effect of which is to redefine the space.

View of the columns which frame the reception area, realised in steel sheeting and constituting one of the most representative elements of the shop. (C3, D4)

Above the parquet a mirror hangs suspended allowing for a multiplication of the images in unsuspected directions. The difference between a wooden and a carpeted surface marks out the specialisation of the clothing and footwear areas.

The whole is enveloped by a diffuse illumination, based on three stage rails with spotlights. The materials used for the finishes, metal, masonry, wood or concrete, are repeated throughout the premises, helping to define the spaces without the need to revert to partitions.

The treatment of space is based on the substitution of formal division for a species of itinerant or natural sweep. The different functional areas are distributed in a manner that escapes the conventional schemes of this type of establishment. Both the architectural and the aesthetic elements fulfil, at every opportunity, the initial proposal, this being to offer an image of a shop that is open and warm, in which product and customer are the most important aspects, over and above an architecture that is rigid and even a little inhuman. Here lies the root of Eduard Samsó's success.

Sbaiz Spazio Moda

Claudio Nardi

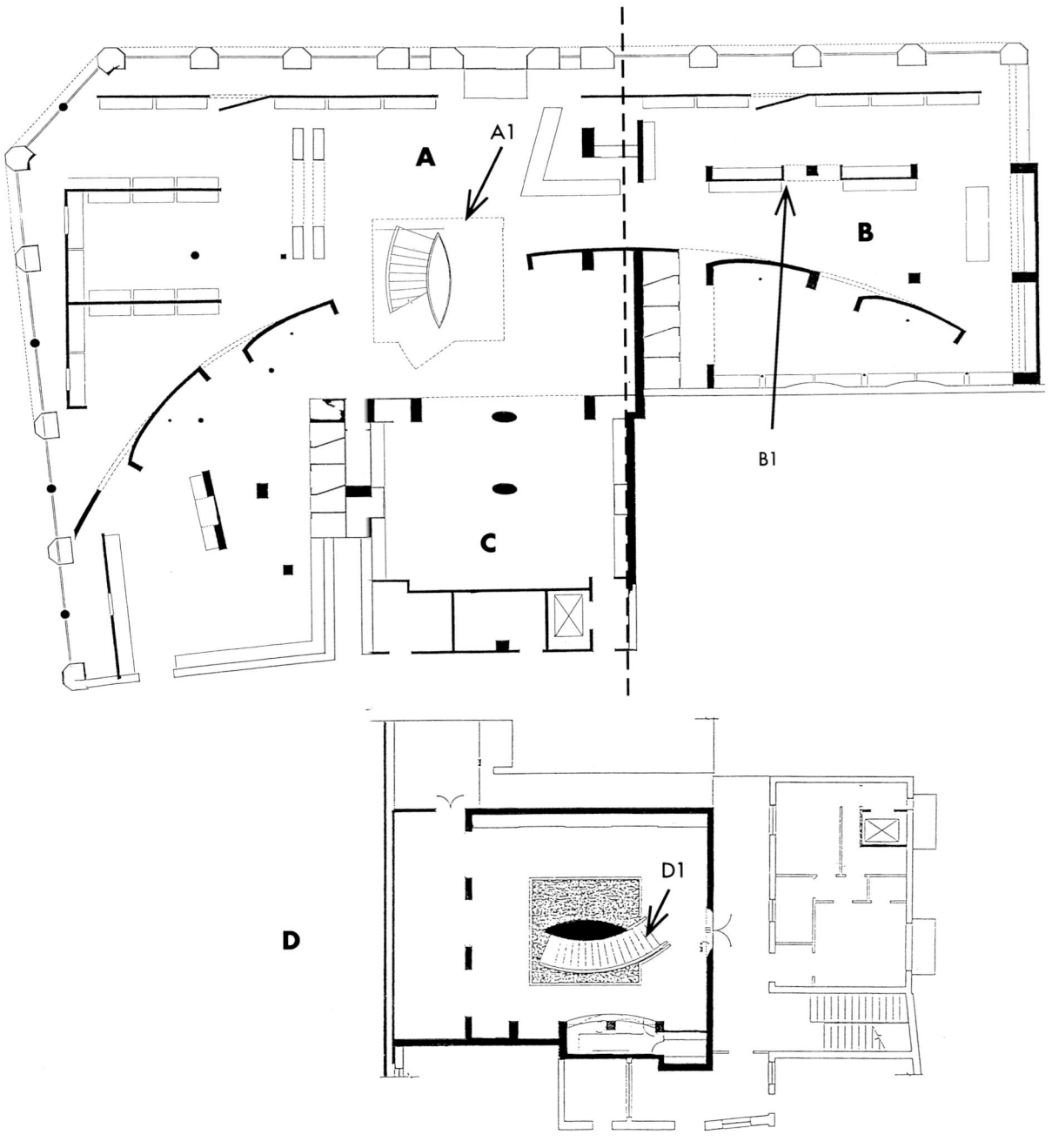

Floor plan of the building, in which we can see the distribution of the distinct areas of the shop, on both floors.

The remodelling of already existing buildings, and the reworking of the façade are often indispensable requirements in many architectural projects. It is not always easy to marry strictly commercial interests, nor those of advertising, to a respect towards the urban environment, in which the building being reformed is to be found. An example of a notable achievement in a case of this type is offered by the realisation of Sbaiz Spazio Moda, a commercial space dedicated to "pret-à-porter", in the Italian town of Ligano Sabbiadora.

The author is Claudio Nardi, who from his studio in Florence has, since 1978, dedicated himself to complex urbanistic projects and small residences, business interiors, offices and public buildings. In the field of architecture he has been responsible for the brilliant restoration of an old country house in Arezzo, the reconstruction of a residence in the historic centre of Ravena, and an office building in Florence. As an interior designer he has designed two bars in this same city, and as an urban planner, he was assigned a project in Roccastrada.

The building on which Nardi's project was realised for the company Sbaiz, was an anonymous construction, a typical exponent of the frenzied real-estate speculation which was experienced in the Italian tourist areas during

Partial view of the ground floor, where the interior remodelling work can be seen, realised on the basis of plaster partitions and columns. (B1)

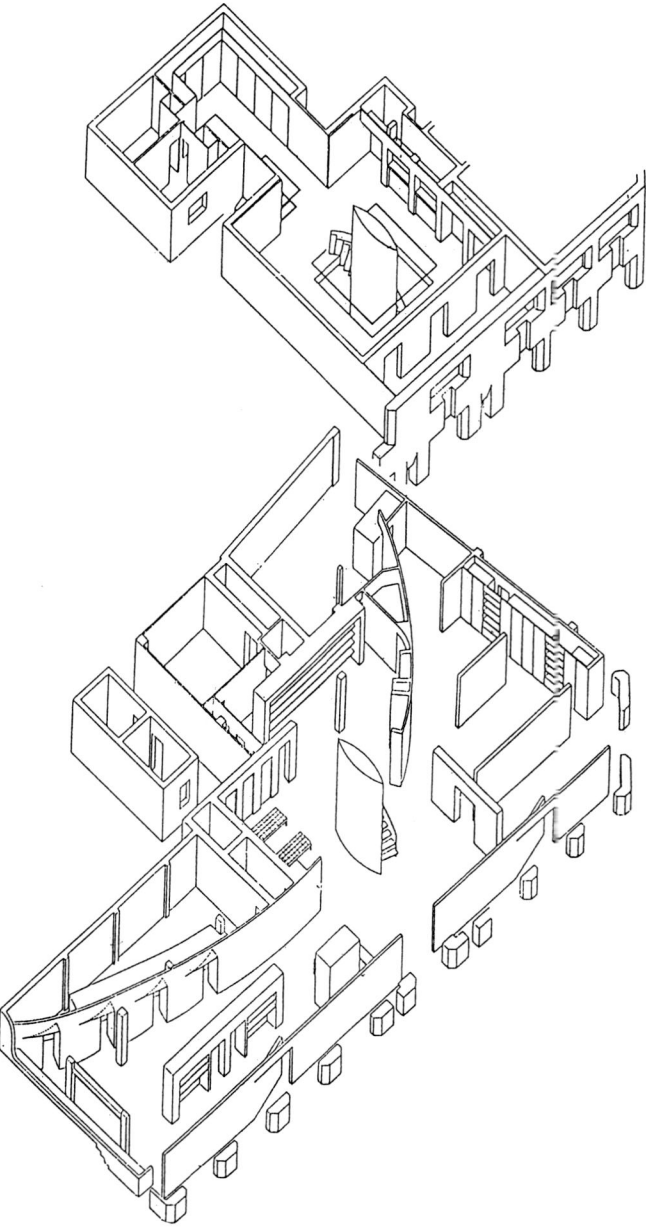

the sixties. The author immediately set-forth the task of remodelling and transforming its overall image.

The first intervention, to the exterior, consisted in the construction of a porticoed gallery, whose roof was a metallic structure at the height of the second floor, and which bordered the whole façade, radically transforming the external perception of the building; the portico and the supporting columns added to the length of the two floors, give it an elegant gracefulness, and also serve to differentiate the commercial space, properly speaking, from the elevation of the third floor, perceived in this way as an almost independent unit.

To continue with the exterior, the subtle work on the surface of the façade, with light and refined materials; varnished woods, and panels treated with linseed oil, gives a new personality to a building which previously was merely anodyne.

Insofar as the interior refurbishment, the final result is a completely new space, as there was originally an excess of working surface area, capable of provoking a visual dispersion, and of thus confusing the basic function of the premises. That function being to induce the act of purchasing. The space was fragmented by means of plaster partitions and columns, and converted into a landscape, of an almost urban scale, walking around the prem-

Elevation plan of the building. On the following page, the spiral staircase, executed in hard wood, which is one of the principal axes of the internal structure of the premises. (A1)

Above, overall image of the ground floor, where the clarity and the purity of line are the predominant note. (B1)

In the detail photo, a system for complementary illumination, on the basis of indirect lighting, which issues from "oeil-de-boeuf", or built in spots. (A)

Below, overall plan of a part of the display window, with its nocturnal illumination.

New perspective of the staircase and details of a few areas of the ground floor, the main nucleus of the shop. (A, B)

ises is like walking around a city, with its latticework of streets opening out into open spaces, or squares, where you can wander around, meet people or buy.

Although the various different areas are differentiated, the whole site reflects a yearning for continuity, achieved thanks to the omnipresent pure white of the ceiling, walls and floor. The neutrality and sobriety provoked by the absence of colour achieve the sought after effect: to emphasise the commercial function at the expense of gratuitous stylistic display.

The illumination on the ground floor comes from natural light, which filters down from the floor above through the well of the spiral staircase, the authentic vertebral axis of the interior space. For the other areas there is an indirect and diffuse illumination from a few strategically located spots.

The reduced third floor houses a small art gallery, in which the public can approach the cultural references of the world of fashion.

Nardi has managed, with this project, to establish a species of dialogue between the old and the new, between a façade, rescued from a past without glory, and a harmonious aesthetic, yet at the same time, functional interior.

Diverse images of the redistribution of the original space, on the basis of architectural resources, such as columns and masonry work. (A, C)

On the following page, plan of the second floor of the building, with the stairway in the foreground. (D1)

KENZO

Maurizio Peregalli

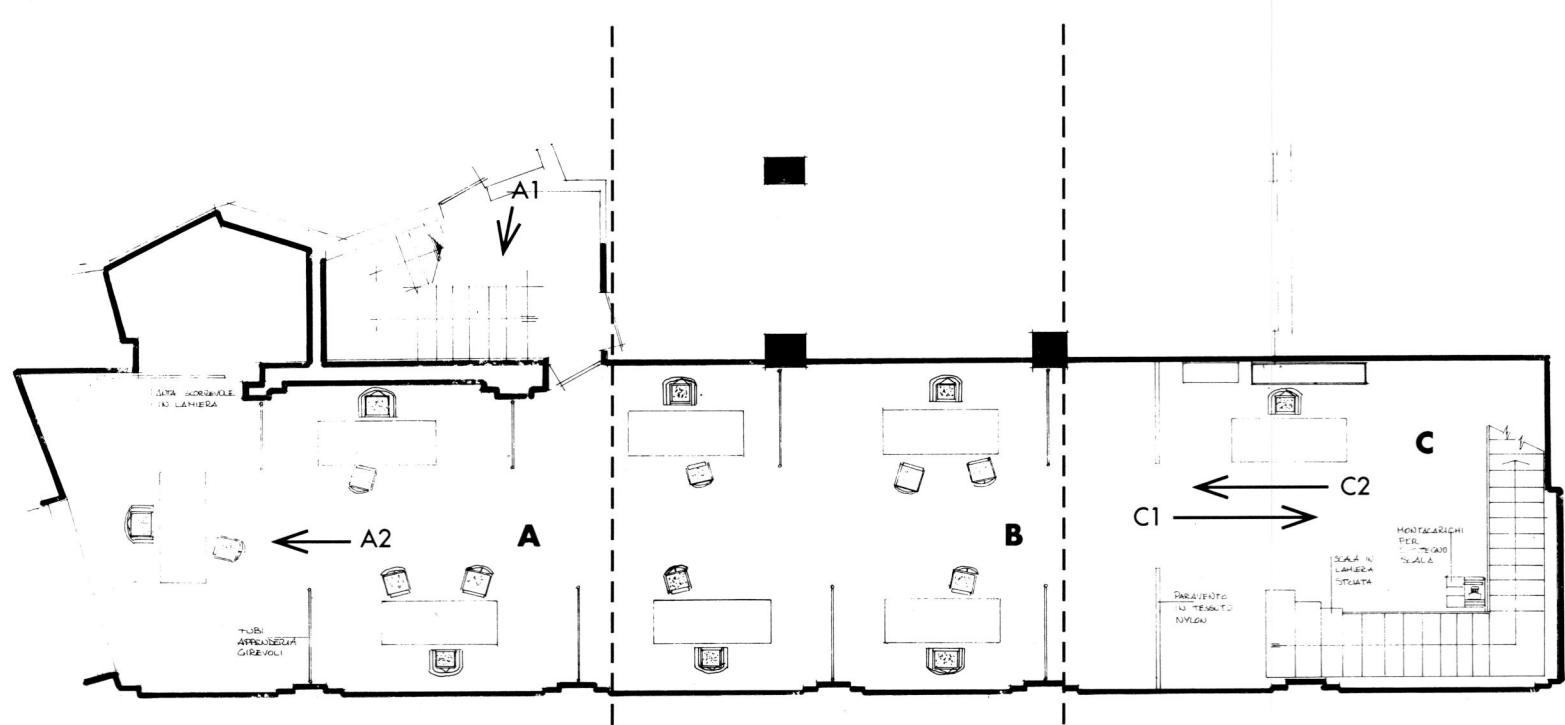

Plan view of the premises and general aspects of the distribution.

Access stairway to the gallery and perspectives of this from above. (A1)

Above, catwalk for the presentations of collections, and below, detail of the back of the establishment. (C1)

Central area of the shop, allocated for attention to the customers. (C2)

Different aspects of the gallery access stairways. (A1)

Details of the distribution of the space and the decoration of the premises. (A)

Following in the same aesthetic line as the Issey Miyake boutique in London, we find the showroom of another Japanese designer, Kenzo, in Milan. With the above denomination, responding to the dominant tendencies in the world of fashion, the definition is sought of a multi-purpose commercial space, this being a place for exhibitions, and at the same time for presenting collections, for models, and also a place which serves as a boutique.

In this type of premises the aim is for the predominance of wide open and comfortable spaces, where the models can be displayed and presentations can occasionally be made. For this reason the presence of shelves and cupboards full of clothes, all of the same model in different sizes, has been avoided. Emphasis is placed on the individual display of different items or combinations, in such a way that their specific characteristics are enhanced.

Maurizio Peregalli, an expert and connoisseur of the world of fashion through his extensive professional experiences, took charge of the Kenzo showroom in Milan. He had been responsible for the design of many of the Giorgio Armani boutiques around the world, in London, Milan and New York. As well as being a designer and interior decorator, Peregalli is also recognised for his furniture designs, a field in which he has had important successes. He is currently in charge of the artistic direction of the design collections of the Italian group Zeus, of which he also happens to be one of the founder members.

The Kenzo project, was constructed on the basis of a large basement type store, long and narrow with a gallery running round it. As the possibility of significant reforms were not being considered, the intervention of the interior designer was reduced to the restoration of certain areas (such as the brick vaults which form the ceiling), white-washing the walls while leaving the rustic surface intact, and renovating the deteriorated flooring with earthenware tiles and quartz grit.

Taking advantage of the shaft of an old hoist an access stairway was installed at one end of the premises. In order to divide the space, revolving panels, perpendicular to the walls, have been employed, from which the displayed clothing is hung. In this way different sales areas have been created, suitable

Area at the back of the establishment, partially allocated for commercial functions. (C)

Main area of the shop, for attention to the customers. (A2)

for the provision of individual attention to the customer, modulating and making the ambience more comfortable. Armchairs and a table, which serves as a counter, have been placed in each of these areas. The entrance area is cut off from the rest of the space by two large semi-transparent panels.

To summarise, this is a precise, one-off performance, which, with just a few brush strokes, has managed to endow the original space with all of the elements necessary for the satisfactory realisation of its commercial function.

SHOWROOM MARCATRÉ

King & Miranda Associati

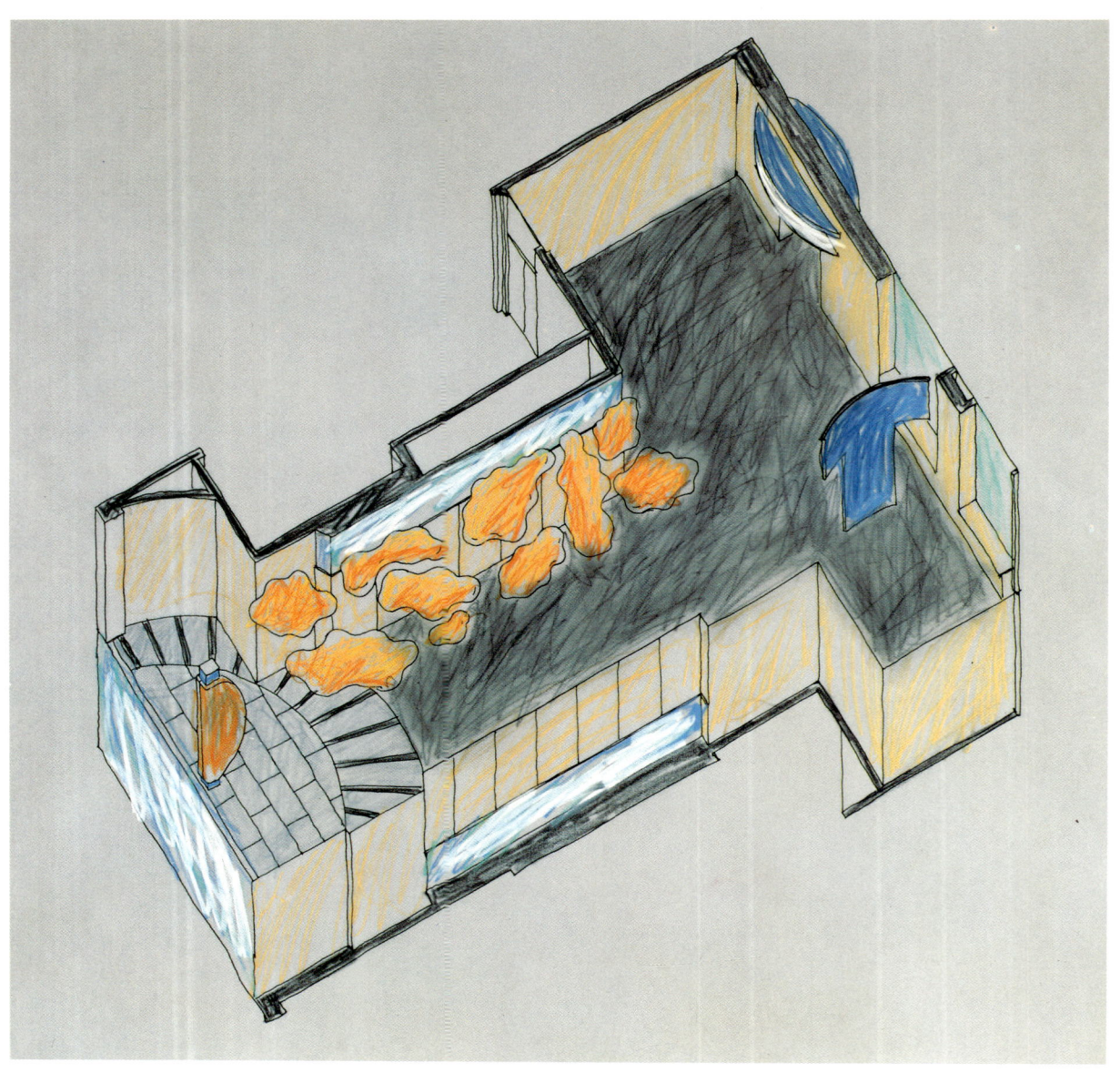

On this page and the following, joint floor and elevation plans, the first just of the entrance area, and the second, of the whole of the premises.

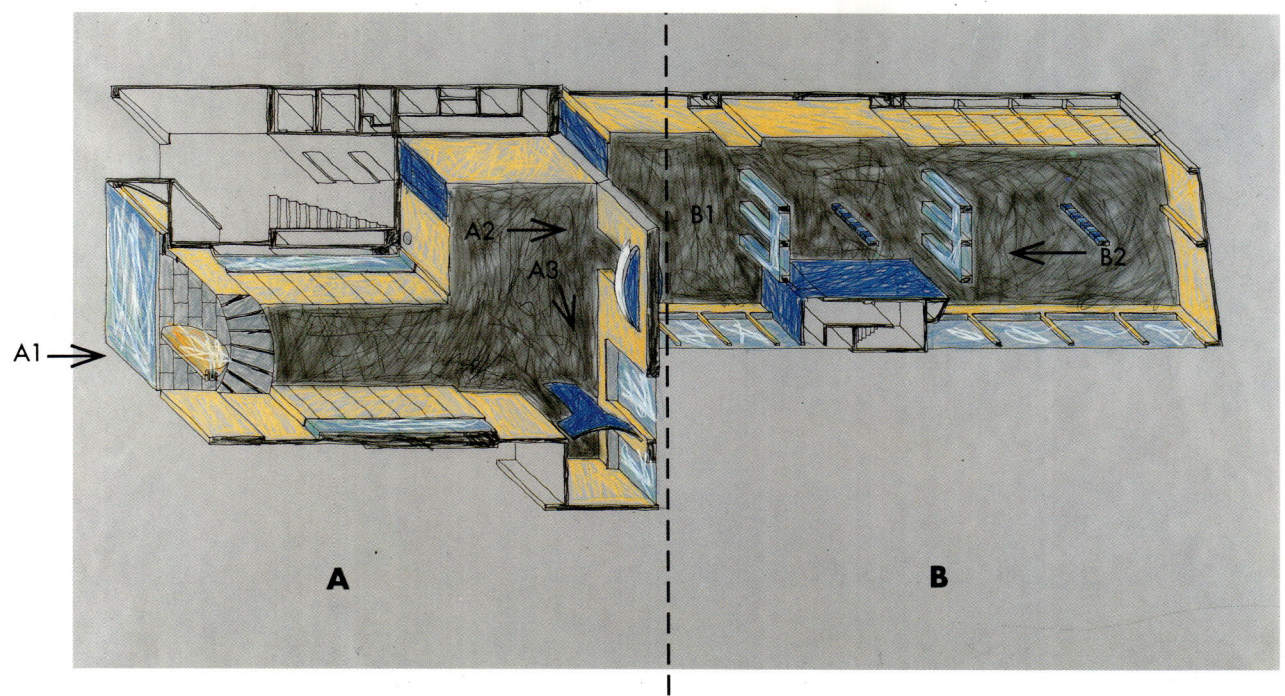

Marcatré, one of the most innovative associations within the office furniture sector, decided to open a new branch store in Paris, in 1989, for which they reverted to their habitual designers, Perry King and Santiago Miranda, the partners of King & Miranda Associati. This studio, founded in Milan in 1976, is involved in all facets of design, whether industrial, interior, or graphic; and the attempt to establish a dialogue between technique and the imagination, as a method of awareness. They have worked for clients in Europe, Japan and the United States, and their work has been recognised on numerous occasions throughout the world.

It was a question of designing a commercial premises, defined as a showroom, removed from the conventionalities that have become associated with ordinary shops. The original space presented a series of structural inconveniences which were adapted and taken advantage of, use being made of them as display areas. The project had to be developed on the site of the ground floor of a relatively new building, made up of a succession of rooms and galleries, projecting diagonally from a small façade looking onto Avenue Hoche.

In these two consecutive photos, the plan of one of the areas, where products are presented to the customers, where we can appreciate the heterogenous volumetry of the premises. (A1)

Aspects of the meeting room, located at the back of the premises, seen respectively from the end of the room and from the entrance. (B1)

The majority of Marcatré's different exhibition premises have been designed with the aim of attempting to reflect the serious and innovative spirit which the company wants to offer to its customers. That is why the intervention of the Italian architects would be directed towards this institutional criteria, and also towards the creation of a cosy working atmosphere (taking into account the offices in the same premises).

The differences in volumes and the heights of the ceilings meant that spatial unity would be lost. As the budget did not allow room for a remodelling of the internal structures, the authors took advantage of this peculiar distribution to organise the different areas for the presentation of the products to the customer, with an independence which would not disturb the rest of the showroom.

This was carried out on the basis of three fundamental premises. Firstly, the original space would have to be transformed and given a new image of extension. Then, following that, visual perspectives would have to be introduced, free from architectural barriers, which would obstruct free circulation and the act of contemplation. Finally the premises would have to be interesting enough to attract the customers inside.

Independent sectors were installed, in such a way that more than creating the divisions, they suggested them. Each area was dealt with in a different and a specific manner, with free forms which border on the artistic. In this sense the conceptual separation has been filled, between the showroom as a premises for exhibition with commercial ends but without direct sales, and the conventionalities associated with a shop.

The premises originally had a glazed façade, which could have been considered as ideal for the main entrance. But finally the option was taken to close off this entrance, and to relocate it in the general lobby of the building. However, the idea of the display window was respected, and a generous exhibition space was allowed for.

For the different functional areas, greater relevance was given to those which were near-

Partial plan of the reception area. (A)

er the street, due to their advantageous location and space, which served to motivate the placing of the main display areas here. The area behind, being of less harmonious proportions was reserved in order to locate the entrance, from the general lobby of the building, and also the company's offices.

With this project, for Marcatré, King & Miranda Associati have ensured their continued progression in the field of interior design, basing themselves on that perfect understanding of volumes and spaces, which helped them to distribute the different functional areas with a complete naturalness. The plastic language of the authors has been developed in freedom, naturally and smoothly dividing the sectors of the original structure, so as to convert them into spaces where architecture, design and art have been fused for one single objective: to favour the act of contemplation, an essential component of the act of buying.

Different images of the area set aside for offices and customer presentations.

Photo above (A2) and photo below. (A3)

Image of the spectacular translucent glass portico, which envelops the two pillars, and from the interior of which emerges a tenuous illumination, instilling a gentle and relaxing atmosphere. (B2)

159